Drink Thy Wine with a Merry Heart

Drink Thy Wine with a Merry Heart

KENNETH MacDONALD

TOM THROCKMORTON

The Iowa State University Press / Ames

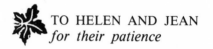 TO HELEN AND JEAN
for their patience

©1983 The Iowa State University Press. All rights reserved. Composed and printed by The Iowa State University Press, Ames, Iowa 50010.

Cover photograph by Tom Throckmorton.

First edition, 1983

Library of Congress Cataloging in Publication Data

MacDonald, Kenneth, 1905–
I.   Throckmorton, Tom, 1913–
     Drink thy wine with a merry heart.

     1.   Wine and wine making.   2.   Wine tasting.
II.   Title.
TP548.M16   1983   641.2′22   82–25852
ISBN 0-8138-0476-0

C O N T E N T S

*Eat thy bread with joy
and drink thy wine with a merry heart.*

—ECCLES. 9:7

FOREWORD

HOW and why two native Iowans got together to write a book about wine puzzled me until I read a few chapters, got into tune with the authors, and then rushed through the remainder of the text. It became clear to me that this book is a labor of love. Enthusiasm, good cheer, and a pervasive mood of gentle humor let you know that the authors are having fun writing of their experiences with wine.

You will find the flow of language easy to read, and the subject matter easy to understand. The authors, like Shakespeare, know that "brevity is the soul of wit." Learn more about wine by reading this pleasant book.

As members of the Iowa Wine Advisory Board, Dr. Tom Throckmorton and Kenneth MacDonald serve without pay, and must not have any conflict of interest. You can be sure that their recommendations of any wines are as impartial as is humanly possible.

This is a book for all lovers of wine. It will help you to understand wine as a social beverage provided for us by the Creator of the microscopic yeast cell, which converts natural grape sugars into the natural alcohol of wine. While thinking of the mysterious nature of fermentation, Benjamin Franklin said "wine . . . a constant proof that God loves us and loves to see us happy."

May your every glass of wine be better than the one you had before.

BROTHER TIMOTHY
Cellar Master
Christian Brothers Winery

P R E F A C E

THIS book is for wine lovers, particularly for those who know little about wine but want to increase their enjoyment of it.

If you already know that Chateau Figeac is a *premier grand cru* of St. Emilion, this book may not be for you. But if you are confused when you walk into a wine shop and see hundreds of bottles on the shelves, if a German wine label is meaningless, if Bordeaux and Burgundy and Beaujolais are merely three words beginning with b, then please read on.

There is little wonder you are confused. In a year's time we and our colleagues on the Iowa Wine Advisory Board have tasted 1,000 different wines, and they were but a fraction of the new wines available. A few were superb, a few were awful, many were so-so, and about a tenth were recommended for stocking in the state's stores.

We are not wine professionals. We do not earn our livelihood making wine or writing about it (one of us is a journalist, the other a surgeon), but over many years we have been visiting vineyards, studying wines, tasting them almost daily, and we hope this book will help others find as much enjoyment of wine as we have.

This book won't make you an expert — only many years of knowledgeable wine tasting will do that — and it won't attempt to tell you which wines you should buy. But it will tell you how to taste with discrimination, what to expect from different types of wine, how to understand labels, how to store your bottles, how to open champagne. It will help you explore the fascinating world of the vineyard and discover for yourself the wines that please you.

KENNETH MACDONALD
TOM THROCKMORTON

Explanations and Acknowledgments

IT may seem strange that a book on wine was written in a state more noted for growing corn than grapes, but Iowans have available an unusually wide selection of wines. Judging from sales, they also have the palates to enjoy them. Stores in the larger Iowa cities carry 700 to 750 different wines, ranging from inexpensive jug wines to the *grands crus* wines of France and the Rhine wines of Germany. Few wine shops anywhere in the United States offer customers as wide a choice. The reason for this abundance is the wine policy established by the state's liquor control council and its director, Rolland Gallagher.

In Iowa all wine and spirits, whether for restaurants, bars, hotels, or home use, must be purchased at stores owned and operated by the state. A Wine Advisory Board assists in the selection of wines for the state inventory. The board tastes and evaluates 1,000 or more wines a year and makes recommendations on purchases. Its seven members are unpaid, and none may have commercial wine connections of any kind.

The idea for this book grew out of the board's weekly tasting sessions, and the lively discussions that characterized those meetings created a hospitable climate for the writing of it. The authors are indebted to their colleagues on the board for help, both direct and indirect. The colleagues are James Lynch, chairman, Alex Ervanian, M.D., Owen Fleming, Diane McComber, Max Rochholtz, and two ex officio members, Mr. Gallagher and Diane Nichols, wine coordinator on his staff.

The authors have relied on a number of books for background information. The following have been most helpful:

Adams, Leon D. *The Wines of America.* (New York: McGraw-Hill, 1978)

Bespaloff, Alexis. *Wine: A Complete Introduction.* (New York: New American Library, 1971)

Churchill, Creighton. *The World of Wines.* (New York: The Macmillan Company, 1964)

Johnson, Hugh. *The World Atlas of Wine.* (New York: Simon and Schuster, 1971)

Kressmann, Edouard. *The Wonder of Wine.* (New York: Hastings House, 1968)

Lichine, Alexis. *New Encyclopedia of Wines and Spirits.* (New York: Alfred A. Knopf, 1978)

Ramey, Bern. *The Great Wine Grapes and the Wines They Make.* (San Francisco: Great Wine Grapes, 1977)

Schoonmaker, Frank. *Encyclopedia of Wine.* Revised by Julius Wile. (New York: Hastings House, 1978)

Schoonmaker, Frank. *The Wines of Germany.* Revised by Peter Sichel. (New York: Hastings House, 1980)

Storm, John. *An Invitation to Wines.* (New York: Simon and Schuster, 1955)

Wagner, Philip M. *Grapes into Wine.* (New York: Alfred A. Knopf, 1979)

All these books are recommended to anyone seeking more information.

The word *we* has been used in two ways in this book. In reporting personal experiences in restaurants and vineyards it has been used as the editorial *we*, a substitute for *I*. In this use the word may refer to the experiences of only one of the authors. In expressing opinions and conclusions, the word has been used in its collective sense, and those statements represent the opinions and conclusions of both authors.

Drink Thy Wine with a Merry Heart

1. The Wine Snob and the Wine Slob. Beware!

 W I N E has been enjoyed for centuries. Its history is full of myths and truths and rituals, and a fair amount of mystery. Although wine making today is as much science as art, no one yet knows precisely why a certain grape under certain conditions becomes a wine that may live and change and give pleasure for decades. The study of wine is fascinating. As with all fascinating subjects, there are some persons who find the atmosphere so heady they turn into snobs. A character in a James Thurber cartoon once observed, "It's a naive domestic Burgundy without any breeding, but I think you'll be amused by its presumption." When you hear talk like that, there is a wine snob at your elbow.

Wine snobs want to be regarded as unusually sensitive about food and drink, more attuned to the good life than you are. They may or may not be sensitive and finely tuned; to them the important point is the impression they create.

The wine cult would insist that you know each vineyard and its history, that you select your wines according to traditional patterns, that bottles be stored at precise temperatures, opened and poured according to precise etiquette. Each wine must be served in a glass shaped for that purpose—one glass for red Bordeaux, another for white Bordeaux, still another for red Burgundy, one glass for Rhine wine, one for Moselle, one for champagne, one for sherry. To entertain eight or ten guests at dinner you would need about seven dozen glasses to be prepared for all occasions.

Wine snobbery is a relatively harmless conceit as long as you recognize it and are not intimidated by it. To enjoy wine you do not need to know every hillside in France and which way it faces. You do not have to memorize the century-old classifications of Bordeaux vineyards. You do not need dozens of glasses.

But there are some things you do need to know. You need to know because there are a multitude of choices, and the choices are constantly changing. Wine, more than anything else you eat or drink, is of infinite variety. If you have a favorite whiskey or gin, you can buy it year after year knowing it will always be the same — unless the sales manager persuades the maker to change the formula. But when this year's XYZ Chablis is gone there won't be any more exactly like it.

The Greek philosopher Heraclitus once said that a man never steps in the same river twice; meaning, of course, that the river is always changing. With only slight exaggeration he might also have said that a person never drinks the same kind of wine twice.

Five things determine the character and quality of a wine — the grape variety, the soil in which it is planted, the weather, the ability of the grower, and the skill of the winemaker. A change in any of these will affect the taste. The amount of limestone or granite or sand or chalk in the soil affects the development of the grape, and it affects different grapes differently. The Pinot Noir grape produces some of the world's greatest wine in the Burgundy region of France near Dijon. A few miles south the same grape makes a less distinguished wine.

A few days more or less of sunshine, a few degrees of temperature change at a crucial time, the amount of rain and when it falls all affect the wine. So sensitive is the grape to climate and soil that two vineyards planted to the same grape on opposite sides of a road may produce slightly different wines. Wine made this year will not be identical with wine made last year by the same winemaker from the same variety of grapes. It may be just as good or better, but it won't be the same.

If you buy two or more bottles of the same wine of the same year and keep them properly in your cellar, perhaps the wines will have identical properties when you drink them. But even then there may be differences. Good wine continues to change in the bottle. If there are long intervals between the times you open the bottles, there will be subtle differences in taste. A fine Bordeaux of the 1975 vintage would have been too young in 1980. A Beaujolais would have been too old.

This does not mean you should not go on drinking wine from a particular vineyard year after year. Responsible winemakers try to maintain quality and consistent taste from year to year, and the differences from one year to the next are often too slight for any one except an expert to detect. Nevertheless, the way to select wines for your greatest enjoyment, from among the hundreds available, is to compare different wines until you know which you like best and can recognize them when you find them. You will do this more confidently if you know a few basic facts about grapes, the regions where they grow best, and the procedures of the winemakers.

This is the reason to beware not only of the wine snob who may be standing at your side but also of the wine slob who may be lurking at your other elbow. He is the person who tells you not to worry about types of grapes or what the label says. Stick with a wine you like, pour it in any type of glass, and drink it with every food. The wine slob is akin to the person who professes not to know anything about art yet insists, "I know what I like."

The purpose here is not to scold. If you like calendar art of a moose silhouetted against a flaming sunset, hang it on your wall and enjoy it. If you enjoy a sweet jug wine with all of your meals, drink it. We defend your right to do both, but the suggestion offered here is that with a little experimentation and a small amount of knowledge you might find a picture more pleasing than that silhouetted moose, and you might find a wine that makes you wonder why you enjoyed Lambrusco so much.

A good wine will taste good in an old peanut butter jar or a paper cup (we have drunk it both ways), but you will enjoy it more in a glass that lets you see its color and sense its aroma. That doesn't mean a glass for every type of wine; it means a fairly large, uncolored, undecorated glass with a slightly smaller circumference at the top (tulip-shaped) to concentrate the aroma.

The wine slob tends to equate wine with booze; the wine snob tends to equate wine with great art. There is a superficial basis for both views, but only superficial. Wine does contain alcohol — it would be thin without it — and if you drink enough of it you will get drunk, but if that's what you want, vodka is quicker. A truly great wine with brilliant color, subtle bouquet, perfect balance, and lingering taste is a sensuous experience and a work of art, but such wines are rare and costly.

Although there is alcohol in wine and artistry in wine making, a better comparison is with food. The French and the Italians, who drink more wine than any other people, do consider it a food and drink it every day as a part of their meals. Like food, wine has endless variety. It may come from an ancient Bordeaux chateau, it may be ordinary table wine, it may be something in between. All wines have their place. Beef can be well aged prime sirloin or ground hamburger. Most people don't eat prime sirloin every day, and few people drink a superb wine every day unless they own the winery. Hamburgers are fine food, but you don't want to eat them every day, either, unless you are nine years old.

The reward for studying wine (and food) is discovering the variety of pleasures available to you. You do this by experimenting with different wines and different foods and by comparing the same types of wines made from different vineyards. Steer a middle course between the self-proclaimed expert, who knows everything (some of which probably isn't true), and the dullard, who is proud of knowing nothing. Strike out on your own. Listen to Winston Churchill. With the survival of his country resting in his hands he found time to be a reasonably good amateur painter. The way to begin, he said, is to pick up the brush, dip it in paint, and attack the canvas.

Buy a few bottles of wine, draw the corks, and start tasting.

2. Tasting

 Y O U drink wine to enjoy the taste. You may drink milk because it is good for you. You may eat vegetables for the minerals they contain. You may eat chicken because it is low in cholesterol. You could drink wine for all of these reasons, too, but you don't; you drink it to enjoy the taste.

There are additional reasons to drink wine, of course — it complements food, it enhances conversation, it adds color and sparkle to the table, and it provides a warm feeling of well-being. But enjoying its taste comes first, and because there is such variety in wine, the ability to taste with sensitivity and discrimination is the key to fullest enjoyment.

Wine should be savored slowly, not gulped like cold lemonade on a summer day. Wine is complex, and the better it is, the more complex it is. It can also be subtle, and the complexities and subtleties will be lost in a fast gulp. Full enjoyment requires the senses of the eyes, the nose, and the mouth.

Ordinarily we think of taste as the sensation that comes with chewing and swallowing, but in tasting wine and many foods as well, the nose is more important than the mouth. Think how food tastes when you have a cold and can't smell. Physiologists remind us that the olfactory nerves can distinguish thousands of different odors whereas our taste buds can distinguish only four qualities — sweet, sour, salt, and bitter. Eyes also have an important function in tasting. Enjoyment of a wine's color increases anticipation and enhances perception. Thus, the flavor of a wine is a combination of

7

all our sensory reactions to colors and smells along with the reaction of our taste buds.

Each person can develop his or her own technique for tasting wine, but there is a procedure that can be recommended, not as a ritual to be followed slavishly (and certainly not ostentatiously in public) but as an effective way to discern a wine's characteristics. Begin by observing the color in the glass. Colors range from deep purple through shades of red, rose, pink to the color of sparkling spring water and on to straw, pale yellow, delicate yellow green, amber, deep gold, brown gold. With experience you will recognize whether the color is right for the wine you are sampling. If there is a tinge of brown in a red table wine, for example, it is a sign of age, perhaps too much age. Note whether the wine is clear, as it should be, or cloudy. Swirl the wine in the glass to release its aroma. Take a few light sniffs and note your reaction, then inhale deeply to get the full aroma. Sip enough wine to cover all of the taste buds, which are located on the tip, sides, and back of the tongue, and give them an opportunity to react. Swallow and exhale through the nose, noting the flavor that seems to fill the mouth and head. You may then want to swallow a larger amount and note the flavor. See if there is a lingering aftertaste, which can be quite different, pleasant or unpleasant, from the first reaction.

Some tasters think the most effective way to experience the full flavor is to draw air into the mouth through the wine before the first sip is swallowed. There is a trick to doing this, but you can learn it with practice. Take a small amount of wine in your mouth, tilt your head forward slightly, open your mouth a bit, and draw in air through the wine. Close your mouth, swallow, and exhale through your nose. Warning: Practice in private before attempting this in public. Until you learn the trick, you may choke. Even when you become adept, it is desirable to limit this procedure to wine tasting sessions with friends or colleagues. If you do it properly, you make a bubbling noise that sounds something like gargling, which dinner guests may not enjoy. This tasting trick is one of many points on which wine experts disagree. Some think drawing in air is ostentatious and futile; others feel they can't taste a wine fully in any other way. Try it and see whether you find it helpful.

Whatever technique you develop, the important point is to concentrate on what your eyes, nose, and mouth are telling you. You will quickly detect whether the wine is sweet or the opposite, dry. The fermentation process changes the sugar in grape juice to alcohol. If the fermentation stops before all of the sugar is converted, the wine will have a sweet taste. It may be only slightly sweet or very sweet. Most red wines tend to be dry except for a few after dinner wines, such as port. White wines vary from very dry to very sweet dessert wines.

If you detect an astringent feeling in your mouth while tasting red wine, it probably is caused by tannin. Tannin comes from the skin of the grape, and the amount of it in a wine depends on how long the skins were left in the juice, or *must*, during processing. It is a necessary ingredient in a red wine that is intended to improve with age, a red Bordeaux, for example. Too much of it when the wine is young can be unpleasant, but if the wine otherwise shows promise, the tannin taste will diminish with age.

You will learn to detect acidity or lack of it, particularly in white wines. Too much acidity is unpleasant, but too little leaves the wine tasting flat. The amount of alcohol will affect the sensation in your mouth. Alcohol itself is tasteless, but your mouth will detect its presence. A wine with too little alcohol will taste thin or watery. A wine with the proper amount will have more "body," and one with too much will taste "hot." In addition to these reactions, you will detect aromas and flavors that come from the various components of the grape. These vary widely depending on the kind of grape, the climate in which it grew, the degree of ripeness when it was picked, and the processing of the must.

Soon you will learn that a wine from a certain grape has a distinctive flavor, as does, for example, a wine made from the Cabernet Sauvignon grape. Once you have identified that flavor you will recognize it whenever you encounter it. And you will also discover that sometimes a wine labeled a Cabernet Sauvignon doesn't taste like one. That is the beginning of discrimination; you will not buy that particular brand again when you are shopping for a Cabernet.

As you taste each wine, try to fix its distinctive characteristics in your memory. Try to describe its flavor to yourself if you are alone or discuss it with friends if several of you are tasting together. For example, most wine drinkers think of Beaujolais as being fruity. Zinfandel reminds some tasters of blackberries. One widely known expert, Alexis Lichine, finds in fine, aged red Bordeaux "a woodland freshness or an earthy smell of low-growing violets." Chardonnay to some people tastes flinty. Some wines have a scent of honey or apples or newly cut hay. Few wines fit these descriptions literally; a little imagination is necessary, but trying to find appropriate adjectives will force you to concentrate and help you remember flavors so you can identify them later.

One member of the Iowa Wine Advisory Board, who has both a sensitive palate and a vivid imagination, makes comparisons that sometimes seem wholly unrelated to wine but have caused others to sip again and look for an elusive flavor they may have missed. The aftertaste of one wine reminded him of talcum powder. The aroma of another had a slight, not unpleasant suggestion of a horse barn! Another member of the board found a hint of sauerkraut in the aroma of one wine, in this case not a pleasant discovery.

As you taste different wines try to determine how one differs from another and why one may seem more pleasing than another. If you are a beginner, however, it is better not to be rigid in selecting your favorites. Your likes and dislikes will change the more you taste. As children we liked simple foods, particularly sweet ones; as we grew older we developed appreciations for more complex and subtle dishes. The beginner is likely to find sweet wines the most pleasing, because most of us like sweets in any form and also because, in inexpensive wines, sweetness tends to mask unpleasant flavors. With more experience the appeal of dry wines will grow. Some of the world's renowned wines are sweet, but most of these are intended for drinking with dessert or without food. Sweetness tends to dull the appetite, which is one reason why sweet foods are usually served at the end of the meal.

Try to decide how each wine you sample would taste with different foods. A sweet Sauternes and a dry red Burgundy are as different as bananas and oranges and are no more susceptible to comparison. The former could be delightful with the dessert, but cloying with the roast beef. The Burgundy would be fine with the meat course, but not very pleasing with baked pears.

So taste carefully and knowingly. Books alone won't make you knowledgeable about wine, although we hope this one will help. Tasting is the only way to learn. During a friendly argument about a wine at a recent tasting session, one panel member defended his position with a quotation from a widely known wine book. "The trouble with you, George," said a colleague, "is that you read too much. You ought to taste more and read less."

The proper course is to do both. Keep on reading but taste, taste, taste.

3. Red or White, Sweet or Dry

 W I N E making is older than recorded history. It is as simple and natural as a sunrise. Before men and women could read or write they discovered that fruit juices, if left alone for a time, fermented, and if they didn't know what fermentation was, they were highly pleased with its results. Once having discovered it they never ceased making use of it.

Some people are fascinated with the mechanical details of their automobiles. Others are bored with talk of carburetors and cylinders. A friend once threatened to walk out of a showroom if the salesman opened the hood. On the assumption that your interest at the moment is drinking wine, not making it, this book will not attempt to instruct you in the process that changes fresh grape juice into wine. Only enough detail will be provided to explain some of the terms used in defining or classifying wines. How the wine is made determines, among a wine's other characteristics, its color, its alcoholic content, and its degree of sweetness. The sweetness determines whether the wine is intended primarily as table wine to be drunk with food or as a dessert wine to be used primarily with the last course of a meal or after the meal.

Wine making today is a science as well as an art. Scholarly research is done on all phases of it. Vintners are trained at universities. Expensive machinery has been designed for harvesting, crushing, fermenting, testing, and bottling. Sophisticated marketing programs are devised by business school graduates, and many wineries are owned by big corporations.

But the basic process is still simple and natural. The grapes are picked and crushed. The juice is allowed to ferment. In fermenting, the sugar in the juice turns into alcohol. And in the process a blend of various tastes is produced — pleasant or unpleasant, simple or complex — depending on the grape, the soil, the sunshine and rain, and the handling of the fermentation.

The juice of most grapes is colorless. If the skins of red grapes are left in the must during fermentation, the wine will be red. If the skins are removed before fermentation, the wine will be white. If the skins are removed at some point during fermentation, the wine will be rose-colored, a rosé. The color of the growing grape does not determine the color of the wine; white wine can be, and is, made from red or black grapes.

Red wines tend to be heavier, more full-bodied, more robust, "chewier" than white wines, although there are exceptions. They also, in general, last longer in the bottle than white wines because of the tannin, which comes from the skins. Tannin can be very noticeable and distracting in a young red wine. However, it disappears with time, and by enabling the wine to live and age in the bottle, it enhances the taste and enjoyment.

White wines tend to be lighter, fresher, more sprightly, more delicate, more short-lived, but here again there are exceptions. There are few absolutes in wine. The possibility of surprise every time a cork is drawn is part of the fascination.

Rosés tend to fall between the reds and whites, and some purists belittle them as characterless and lacking in distinction, but don't dismiss them before you have tried them. A rosé with a thick steak may seem thin and watery, but a cold bottle with a light lunch on a hot summer afternoon can be very refreshing. Rosés somewhat resemble white wines and are sometimes used in the same manner.

If the fermentation process continues until most of the natural sugar has been transformed into alcohol, the wine will be *dry*, meaning not sweet, and it will usually have an alcoholic content between 8 and 14 percent. Because of the dryness and the alcoholic content this wine, whatever its color, is considered table wine. Most experienced wine drinkers do not like a sweet wine with any food except dessert for the same reason that most people would not like chocolate cake with roast beef. An alcoholic content higher than 14 percent usually has a "hot" aftertaste and would be considered too strong to drink with food by most wine lovers, and a content lower than approximately 8 or 9 percent would seem thin or flat.

If the must has a high sugar content and if the fermentation ceases or is stopped before all of the sugar is turned into alcohol, the result will be what is called a sweet wine. A must may be high in sugar because the grapes were picked when overripe, or because of the type of grapes used, or because sugar in some form was added to the must. A sweet wine, such as a French Sauternes, although inappropriate with the main course of a meal, is delicious with many desserts and with pâtés.

Besides adding sugar, there are other ways of altering the must to produce different types of wine. If brandy, which is distilled from wine, is added, the wine develops a much higher alcoholic content and is called *fortified*. Two examples of fortified wines are port and sherry. They can be delightful at the end of the meal. Sherry is also served as an aperitif and with some first courses.

Wines may also be flavored with such substances as herbs and spices, fortified to give them higher alcoholic content, and drunk as aperitifs or in mixed drinks. Vermouth is a popular example. A wine like this made from a private formula may have a proprietary label. Dubonnet is an example. Vermouth, Dubonnet, and other such wines are never considered table wines.

The fermentation process releases carbon dioxide gas, which, in most wine making is released into the air. If some of it is captured and held, the result is an effervescent or sparkling wine. Champagne, real or imitation, is the best known example, but a number of other wines have at least slight effervescence. A slightly effervescent wine is called *petillant* in French, *frizzante* in Italian, and *spritzig* in German. More effervescent wines in Italy are called *spumante*.

There are more than 8,000 varieties of grapes — no one knows the total number. Theoretically some sort of wine can be made from all of them; actually most of it would be undrinkable. Less than a hundred varieties have the right combination of sugar and acids and extractable flavors to produce good wines, and only a handful are capable of being fashioned into really superb wines.

The viticulturalist, the grape grower, has a demanding task, and success requires both skill and luck. Only the grape varieties suitable to the specific soil and prevailing climate should be planted. If superior wine is the objective, the yield must be regulated. Most viticulturalists agree that each vine has the potential to produce a limited amount of the needed elements—sugar, acids, and so on. If the yield is abundant, these compounds are distributed lightly over the full harvest. If the yield is restricted, the same amount of "quality" is concentrated in fewer grapes.

There must be enough rain to provide growth, but not enough to induce rot in closely clustered berries. Cool, foggy nights bring joy; frosts that shrivel and blacken the berries bring despair. Drought can be catastrophic. Insects, mildews, fungus outbreaks, bacteria, and viruses abound and must be dealt with. The warm days of late summer may either swell the grapes into maturity or sunburn the ripening fruits.

All in all, the life of the grape grower is not entirely a happy one, but when superb grapes from superior varieties are brought to the crusher at exactly the proper time and in the proper condition, the result can be happy indeed for everyone.

4.   Grapes — the Noble Four

 S U N S H I N E, rain, soil, skill — each is necessary to produce a good wine, but it is the grape variety that chiefly determines a wine's characteristics. To oversimplify a bit if you know the grapes, you know the wine. This and the two following chapters will list the major wine grapes and explain briefly what kind of wine each grape produces. More than forty different grapes will be described. That may be more detail than you want to absorb in one sitting, but this cataloguing will provide an easy reference when you want to learn the characteristics of any wine you are likely to find available in this country. The four most important grapes in wine making are described in this chapter. Chapter 5 covers the other grapes used in Europe and the western United States. Chapter 6 describes native American grapes and the hybrids used in the eastern United States.

There are two broad categories of wine grapes, the so-called European grapes and the American grapes. The former were first cultivated in Europe, but are now also widely planted on the West Coast of the United States. All European wines and 80 to 90 percent of American wines are made from varieties of the European grapes. If you are interested in botanical names, the European grapes are all varieties of the species *Vitis vinifera,* the most important species in wine making.

The European grapes do not grow well in the eastern United States where the winters are cold. Eastern winemakers, therefore, have relied heavily on the American wine grapes. These varieties are native to the eastern seaboard; they were there when the first white settlers arrived. They are varieties of two other species, *Vitis labrusca* and *Vitis rotundifolia.*

There was a time when all of the world's best red wines and the best whites except Rieslings and Tokays came from France. Thus, the best of the French became the standard by which other wines were judged. Traditions grew up around the historic French vineyards, some of which had been in existence before the Europeans discovered America, and their names became synonymous with great wine. These names still stand as symbols of quality, but today California wines can be superb, too, and in some categories, equal or superior to the French. It is likely you will be buying more wine produced in California than in Europe—it is good, it is generally cheaper, and it is more available—but the grape descriptions that follow will include enough information on European wines to familiarize you with some of the great traditional names and to guide you to a superb bottle.

Any description of wine grape varieties should begin with the four noble grapes, so-called because under ideal growing conditions and skillful handling, they can produce the best wines in the world. All are European varieties. Two are red, Cabernet Sauvignon and Pinot Noir. Two are white, Chardonnay and Riesling.

Cabernet Sauvignon

This grape makes most of the greatest red wines in the world, the Bordeaux wines of France (sometimes called Claret in England), and the best red California varietals, those labeled Cabernet Sauvignon. (A wine labeled with the name of the grape variety from which it was made is called a varietal wine.) The grape's only rival is the Pinot Noir, which does not fare as well throughout the world.

The Cabernet Sauvignon is a vigorous vine that produces grapes sparingly. Its berries are small, flavorful, and thick skinned, with an abundance of both pigment and tannin. It follows that the wines are deeply colored, aromatic, and rich, with sufficient tannin to live in the bottle for long periods.

Bordeaux is the home of this grape, and the *grands crus* (great growths) wines from this region are its finest expression. The great wine chateaux, surrounded by beautifully tended vineyards, lie along the southwest bank of the Gironde River in the Medoc district. The soil of deep gravel is lean, but these grapes are at their best when stressed. The scientists will have to explain why it is that the "easy life" makes fat grapes with little character. The world famous chateaux of Lafite-Rothschild, Latour, Margaux, Mouton-Rothschild, and Haut Brion form a magnificent showcase for Cabernet Sauvignon, and there are several dozen other chateaux that do not suffer badly by comparison.

Comparable wines are to be found in several areas of California. Among the many vineyards that produce marvelous vintages from this grape are Joseph Phelps, Burgess, Heitz, Clos du Val, Beaulieu, Caymus, Chateau Montelena, Diamond Creek, Robert Mondavi, Mayacamus, Ridge, Stag's Leap Wine Cellars, Spring Mountain, Jordan, Conn Creek, and Villa Mount Eden.

Cabernet Sauvignon wines, by and large, are meant to be "laid down" and allowed to age. If tasted early, the wealth of tannin will hide the underlying fruit, body, and complexity of the wine. But the tannin acts as a preservative, and as it yields to time the glorious bouquets and tastes emerge. This may take five, ten, or twenty years. And sadly, it may never occur, and the wine becomes only a bridesmaid.

Many Cabernet Sauvignon wines are tempered, or rounded off, by adding measures of wines from the Merlot or Cabernet Franc grapes to the finished product. Cabernet Sauvignon wines are full and majestic, but the wines made of Merlot grapes have a supple softness and marvelous bouquet that smooth most Bordeaux wines and add a dimension to their "nose."

Merlot is widely grown in the Pomerol and St. Emilion districts of the Bordeaux region and is the primary grape in the wines of some of the great chateaux there, which include Petrus, Cheval Blanc, and Vieux Chateau Certan.

Merlot is also frequently used in Cabernet Sauvignon bottlings in California, and some Merlot is occasionally marketed there as a varietal. If you want to taste Merlot and your purse is too thin for Chateau Petrus, try a California bottle from Joseph Phelps or Clos du Val.

Like Merlot, Cabernet Franc is used primarily as an additive to Cabernet Sauvignon bottlings. It might be described as the Beaujolais grape of the region. Its wines are full of fruit and add good measure to the austere Bordeaux. Also made from the Cabernet Franc grape, outside of Bordeaux, are the lovely soft, fruity red wines of the Loire Valley region, Chinon and Bourgueil.

Cabernet Franc wines are not widely produced in California,

but you will be well rewarded by sampling a bottle produced by Mike Bernstein of the Mount Veeder Winery.

In California several variations based on the Cabernet Sauvignon have appeared; wines labeled Cabernet Rosé or Cabernet Sauvignon Blanc are two examples. Our recommendation: Avoid them until you are familiar with the standard Cabernet Sauvignons.

Pinot Noir

This grape of the Burgundy region in France is the second noble red grape. The vines are of only moderate vigor and of low to modest productivity. The grapes are extremely seedy, their thick skins deeply pigmented.

The Pinot Noir reaches its epitome in the Cote d'Or (golden slope) district of Burgundy, a great curving hillside that descends from a wooded escarpment to the Saone River valley. It begins south of Dijon, runs south for about thirty miles—sometimes a mile wide, sometimes only a few hundred yards—and contains the finest Pinot Noir vineyards in the world. These surround such famous villages as Vosne-Romanee, Nuits-St.-Georges, Aloxe-Corton, Beaune, and Pommard. The greatest concentration of notable Burgundy wines lies adjacent to the tiny village of Vosne-Romanee. It has been said, and rightly, "there are no bad wines from Vosne." Within the reach of an arrow from a well-drawn bow, are wines named La Romanee, Romanee-Conti, Richebourg, La Tache, Romanee-St.-Vivant, Grand Echezeaux, Echezeaux, Clos de Vougeot, Les Suchots, and Aux Malconsorts. Other great Burgundy wines include Chambertin, Musigny, and Corton. If the *grands crus* wines from Bordeaux are the kings of red wines, then certainly these are the queens.

The Burgundy wines are lighter in color than the Bordeaux, with a distinctive subtle, silken smoothness. Their tannin content is lower than that of the great Cabernet Sauvignon wines, and their lasting powers are somewhat less. A typical Burgundy wine is not a great, dark, heavy thing; it is almost feminine, delicate and exquisitely fine. How does one describe the bouquet and taste of a fine Burgundy? To us its ripe fruitiness is displayed against a faintly musty background, which is not disagreeable, but rather like a grandmother's attic on a sunny afternoon. Some of its musty-fruity aroma enters its taste, as if a whole vineyard had been squeezed into a bottle on some warm early autumn afternoon.

The wines have ample viscosity and alcohol, and they produce great "legs" when swirled in the glass. As they age, a tinge of brown can be seen at the edge of the wine when it is tilted against a light background.

The vineyards of the Cote d'Or are far different from the expansive hectares of the Bordeaux area. They are almost tiny, with a multitude of owners who claim only a few acres each. Clos de Vougeot, a famous vineyard and home of the Confrerie des Chevaliers du Tastevin, a prestigious wine organization, consists of 124 acres held in ownership by about 60 persons. Each owner has his plot, and he plants and tends his own vines. The ages of the vines vary as do the art and skill of the many winemakers. These wines are dispensed through many channels, and yet any of them may appear on the *carte de vin* (wine list) as a Clos de Vougeot.

The world supply of Romanee-Conti comes from a scant 4.5 acres; Romanee-St.-Vivant comes from 23.6 acres with multiple owners. Thus, it is important to know the name of the shipper of Burgundian wines. Certain houses, such as Comte de Vogue, Latour, Bouchard Pere et Fils, Leroy, Domains de Romanee-Conti, and Faiveley among others, have established reputations for sound, well-made wines.

During the last several decades, many Burgundian winemakers have shortened the vinification process to produce lighter wines for earlier consumption. This pervasive practice has resulted in wines of lesser merit and made it more difficult to select Burgundy wines worth the high price they command.

The Pinot Noir grape has a very sensitive disposition, and moving it even a few miles away from the Cote d'Or often results in a wine that is undistinguished and of little interest. Moving the grape to the United States has produced nice, fruity wines here and there, but nothing equaling the taste of the luxuriant wines of Burgundy.

However, some exquisite Pinot Noir wines may be just over the California horizon. Perceptive California vintners are adjusting to the fickle grape. Instead of trying to force its wine to become a Burgundy, they are striving for a unique and desirable product with a destiny of its own, a California style of Pinot Noir wines with intense fruit and enough acid to strike a charming balance. Excellent samples of these varietals may be had from Caymus Vineyards, Firestone, Hoffman Mountain Ranch, Joseph Swan, Villa Mount Eden, Santa Cruz Mountain, and others. Try a few bottles, experiment a bit, and find which ones are to your taste. *Chacun a son gout,* as the French say, "each to his own taste."

The Pinot Noir is a multipurpose grape. It is the backbone of the champagne industry. When grown in the area of Epernay in the Champagne region well north of the Cote d'Or, the early harvested Pinot Noir grapes yield a unique white juice that is hig n acid and relatively so in sugars. As the grapes are crushed and the deep purple black skins immediately removed, a fresh white must results, which is the basic ingredient of most champagnes. After fermentation and blending with white wines from Chardonnay and occasionally Pinot Blanc grapes, a cuvee, or blended lot, that is the basic wine of champagne results. The white grapes add finesse and delicacy, but the Pinot Noir brings the flavor and sugar that balance the higher acidity of the white varieties. The cuvee is bottled, refermented to produce bubbles, and champagne results.

In California, Domaine Chandon is using the Pinot Noir in its champagne making operation. However, even in this instance, the grape is troublesome. The thick, deeply pigmented skins bleed a bit of their coloring into the must if subjected to a little heat. If the grape is picked in cool weather, a lovely white must that becomes brut (dry) champagne is obtained; but if picked and crushed on a warm day, a rosé wine results no matter how quickly the skins are removed. This wine results in the Domaine Chandon Blanc de Noir (white wine from black grapes), a bronzy pink champagne of unique flavor.

We have a friend who constantly battles the inroads of wildlife, especially snails, in his garden. Speaking of escargot he once said, "Give a Frenchman a pest, and he'll eat it." Give a Frenchman a problem Pinot Noir, and he will turn it into a lively and different champagne.

The Caymus Winery in California makes a nonsparkling Pinot Blanc de Noir now labeled Eye of the Partridge. Several other California wineries are bottling bronzy Pinot Noir wines, and they make a handsome chilled accompaniment to a luncheon.

Chardonnay

Often incorrectly called Pinot Chardonnay (it is not a Pinot), this grape makes a greater diversity of wines than any other grape, all of them noteworthy. In France it is the grape of *blanc de blanc* (white wine from white grapes) champagnes. It is also the grape of the great white Burgundies, Chablis, Meursault, and Montrachet, and of the lesser but still good white burgundies, Maconnais Blanc and Pouilly-Fuisse. In America it produces the outstanding California white wines labeled Chardonnay. Small amounts of Chardonnay wine are made under various labels in the temperate regions of New York State.

Chardonnay is a vigorous grower but a shy bearer. It does best in cool locations. In the north of France in the Champagne region, it is the principal grape blended with the Pinot Noir to add delicacy and elegance to the basic wines. *Blanc de blanc* champagnes made solely from Chardonnay grapes are the loveliest of champagnes, light, fresh, expensive. Those champagnes declared vintage wines are often *blanc de blancs.*

Farther south in the Burgundy region, the Chardonnay grape grows around the little village of Chablis and produces wines that are hard, bone-dry with a flinty quality. If you were a Boy Scout it is easy to imagine a wine with the aroma and taste of flint. Try starting a fire with flint and steel. As the piece of steel file or the back of the Boy Scout knife strikes sparks from a flint, there is a pungent, smoky, volcanic odor that soon radiates as a taste. That is the nose and background taste of a great Chablis, with here and there highlights of fruitiness welling up into a long, long aftertaste.

The vineyards and winemaking procedures are the usual Burgundian story of small, widely separated plots, ranging from two to twenty-two acres, each one worked and vinified differently. It is little wonder that most Chablis wines are sold under various shipping firms' labels. There are seven *grands crus* vineyards, which total only about ninety acres. These wines are sold with the vineyard name on the label: Blanchots, Valmur, Les Clos, Vaudesir, Les Preuses, Grenouilles, and Bourgos. No one can explain why these wines are better than those from grapes cultivated fifty yards away, but they are. Something in the soil? The angle or exposure to sunlight? These great Chablis wines are a yellow-gold tinged with green. The typical flint nose will identify them at once, as will the elegant, rich-dry taste.

The Chardonnay grape now skips southward to alight again in tiny plantings on the Cote d'Or north of Beaune at Corton-Charlemagne and Musigny. A magnificent Corton-Charlemagne is at least the equal of any other white Burgundy wine. Exceedingly rare, it is a big wine of golden color with a hint of the northern Chablis steel and a suggestion of the big fruity white Burgundies farther south.

Still farther south on the Cote d'Or where the chalky, rough soil is ideal for the Chardonnay grape are the great plantings of Meursault. Here the wines have lost all signs of their northern hardness and have become full, round, and softly opulent; the French call them fleshy. The bouquet is enchanting: some say like violets; others, like almonds; we say like Meursault.

The Meursault vineyards are among the largest in Burgundy, nearly 2,000 acres, which make 200,000 gallons of wine annually. The *premiers crus* (first growths) carry both the Meursault name and the vineyard's: Perrieres, Charmes, Genevrieres, Boucheres, and others. It is the same grape used to make Chablis, but to compare Meursault and Chablis is to compare oranges and apples.

Farther south lie the vineyards of Montrachet. Here, on a thin chalky soil, are grown the Chardonnay grapes from which are made some of the world's most renowned white wines, great golden wines filled with layers of flavor to the point that one is almost bewildered by the exploding and unforgettable aftertastes. The French call them *formidable*! The vines cover less than twenty acres and the production is dwindling to less than 5,000 gallons annually — to supply an entire world.

Partially surrounding Montrachet are Chevalier-Montrachet and Batard-Montrachet. In certain vintages some believe these wines equal or surpass Montrachet. In any event they, too, are marvelous wines and difficult to come by. Their intensity is spectacular. Lesser but still elegant wines are made from grapes growing close to Puligny and Chassagne. It is allowable to add the village name to the Montrachet names. They are good but high priced for their value.

South of the Cote d'Or near Macon, the Chardonnay grape produces good, plain white wine, the Macon blancs. A few miles farther south is the land of Pouilly-Fuisse. The name looks unpronounceable, but Americans have learned to rattle it off with such ease that bottles of the wine that once cost about $2 now sell for up to $20. Pouilly-Fuisse is a clean tasting, pale yellow, refreshing wine with most of the good qualities of the grape but none of its greatness, a quaffing luncheon or cold-bottle-and-bird picnic wine. Its life span is short.

After following the growth pattern of the Chardonnay grape south through France, it is appropriate to see how it is faring in the United States, particularly in California. And it is faring fantastically well. This is one variety of the European, or *vinifera,* grapes that frequently outdoes its French siblings when properly grown and vinified in America. The average Chardonnay wine, labeled as a varietal wine from Napa, Sonoma, Mendocino, Alexander Valley, Monterey, or Santa Cruz in California is a far better wine than the average French Chardonnay. And the truly great and expensive American Chardonnays are impossible to distinguish from the superb white wines of the Cote d'Or. We have tasted on more than one occasion enormous, sound, and aromatic Chardonnays from California that can be unhesitatingly equated with those from Montrachet, and that is a strong statement.

We remember a Mount Veeder 1975 Chardonnay, a mouth-filling wine competitive with any recent Montrachet. The flint and steel of a Chablis are much more difficult to find in California, but we have had an Alexander Valley Vineyard Chardonnay that, tasted with eyes shut, could have convinced us it was a Chablis.

There are other lovely, exquisitely formed Chardonnays from the smaller California wineries—Roudon-Smith, Far Niente, Jekel, Spring Mountain, Chalone, Acacia, Chateau St. Jean, Chateau Montelena, Keenan, Long Vineyards, Sterling, Ventana, and Clos du Val. They can stand side by side and glass by glass with their French counterparts.

If you have status to maintain and a fat purse, go French. Otherwise, if the situation calls for a graceful long-tasting wine, don't forget the California varietal Chardonnays.

Riesling

The Riesling is the great white wine grape of Germany, which has been transplanted to most of the wine-producing areas of the world. Its finest expression is in the magnificent Rheingau and Moselle wines of Germany, but it also produces fine wines in California and New York, the Alsace region of France, Austria, Switzerland, Italy, and Chile and other South American countries. Its wines can vary greatly—sweet in Germany, dry in France. In America this grape is called the White Riesling or Johannisberg Riesling to distinguish it from other grapes sometimes referred to as Riesling.

The grapes are greenish yellow and lightly speckled. Because the grapes are thin skinned, the northernmost vineyards of Europe would seem inhospitable for this variety, but that is where it does best. The prime vineyards are on south-facing precipitous slopes along the Rhine and Moselle rivers.

The Rheingau region along the Rhine River west of Wiesbaden is almost one uninterrupted vineyard planted mostly to the Riesling grape. It is a counterpart of the French Cote d'Or. And, as in the case of Burgundy, out of almost 3,000 growers, at least 1,000 own less than 1 acre each. Few more than 200 own plots larger than 5 acres. However, a semblance of order was brought out of this viticultural chaos by the 1971 German wine laws. These decreed that no single vineyard should be less than 12.5 acres in size. Neighbors grouped their outputs by vineyard names associated with about 20 villages, as in Burgundy.

Village or vineyard names associated with superb Rheingau wines include Hattenheim, Hallgarten, Rauenthal, Markobrunn, and Erbach. The great Schloss (castle) wines are Johannisberg, Reinchartshausen, Vollards, and Eltz. Among other regions making Rhine wines of varying attractiveness are Rheinpfalz (or Palatinate) and Rheinhessen. If price is of secondary importance, we would recommend the Rheingau wines over the others.

The wines of the Moselle and its tributaries, the Saar and the Ruwer, are the other exceptional German wines made from the Riesling grape. The Moselle arises in France and wanders into Germany, where it finally joins the Rhine at Koblenz. Vineyards of varying quality lie along its banks, producing better wines when on a steep slope with a southern exposure. The soil is largely slate and shale, and the grape thrives on it. The Middle Moselle, from Trier to Zell, is the area of finest wines. The village names identify the wines in general: Piesport, Bernkastel, Wehlen, Graach, Zeltingen, Brauneberg, and Urzig are among the best known.

The vineyard name is a still more accurate indication of quality. Bernkasteler Doktor indicates one of the best-known Moselle wines. It is said that the Bishop of Trier in the fourteenth century was at death's door, losing ground to a strange illness. After drinking a few bottles of Bernkasteler wine, however, he miraculously recovered and lived another ten years. He proclaimed the wine the world's greatest doctor — and who is to argue? The name stuck to the vineyard, an advertising person's dream.

The Moselle wines are soft and light, and their magnificent

floral-fruit aroma makes a mouth-watering bouquet. The taste is that of a great Rheingau Riesling, but with a less formal, lighter disposition. If you need help in identification, the Moselle bottles are tall and green, and the Rhine bottles, tall and brown.

Riesling wines may vary from a light sparkling greenish yellow to a full amber hue, the sugar and extract content increasing with the color. The label will indicate in general what may be anticipated. German wines are classified not by vineyard, but by must weight; that is, the amount of sugars in the juice to be fermented. Advancing degrees of ripeness usually make for more sugar and better quality wines. The sugar content is occasionally increased by outbreaks of *Botrytis cinerea,* that same benign mold responsible for the unique French Sauternes. The mold penetrates the thin skin of the berries. The berries shrink, causing a concentration in the juice and a change in the sugars and other components. Wines made from these shriveled, moldy, raisined grapes are exquisite, among the world's outstanding dessert wines.

Once in a great while, superripe Riesling grapes are caught by a sudden freeze. If crushed while frozen, the water content is greatly reduced, and a fuller, sweeter wine may be produced. Such wines are known as *Eisweins* (ice wines). They are expensive oddities and, just between us, usually of lesser quality than many a German wine produced by less drastic means.

Most German wines are sweet and floral. They are drunk for the pleasure of the wine itself and are seldom an accompaniment to food. Germans often drink beer with meals and wine before or after.

The Riesling grape is successfully grown in the Alsace region of France, but the wines made in that region are far different from the lush wines of the Rhine and Moselle river valleys. Vinified in the French manner, the resulting wines are bone-dry, spicy, and flavorful, and they make attractive table wines. Perhaps these wines are the "Chablis" of the Riesling grape.

The Riesling grape is cultivated with considerable success in California, especially in the cooler regions. We remember with great pleasure tasting a line-up of seventeen Rieslings one morning at Chateau St. Jean, and before breakfast! Any one of the thick, luscious golden amber wines would have made a Germanic heart leap for joy. These are great, truly spectacular wines, of varying character but enormous appeal.

Some dryer wines are now being made in both Germany and

California from the Riesling grape. We recall a "vertical" tasting at Robert Mondavi's, where wines of several different years were tasted from the oldest to the youngest. As we progressed toward the present, the wines became lighter, dryer, with a crisp fruitiness in the mouth — obviously a move toward producing a Riesling compatible with white meats and seafood. Some fine Rieslings of this type are coming from western Oregon, Washington, and Idaho. New York State also is producing a few.

The word *Riesling* is loosely applied in wine nomenclature. The white Riesling described above is the true Riesling. At least four other grapes, listed below, have Riesling as a part of their name.

EMERALD RIESLING. This is a hybrid grape, a cross between white Riesling and Muscadelle developed at the University of California at Davis. The variety has high productivity and, when vinified, adds the Muscat flavor and perfume to the breeding and acidity of the Riesling. The hybrid variety was accepted very slowly in the California world of wine, but today more than 3,000 acres are planted to Emerald Riesling. It makes unique wines. Probably the best known is made by Paul Masson and labeled with the proprietary name of Emerald Dry. The wine is tart, aromatic, lively, and tasty. Some day at San Francisco's Fisherman's Wharf, have a bottle with a Dungeness crab salad. A real value!

FRANKEN RIESLING. This is another name sometimes used for the Sylvaner grape. It is not a true Riesling. The Sylvaner grape is described in the next chapter.

GREY RIESLING. This is not a Riesling grape; it is the Chauche Gris grape of the Charente area of France. It is so little regarded in France that it is never used in the highest quality wines with officially controlled place names. However, it is a strong, high-yielding variety, and it gained a foothold in California, where it gives soft, undistinguished wines with considerable popularity. As a clean, honest, inexpensive, "everyday" wine, it apparently has found a niche from which better low-cost wines have failed to dislodge it.

MISSOURI RIESLING. Not even remotely related to the Riesling grape. It probably derives from a native American variety.

5. Grapes—the Other Europeans

 M O S T of the finest table wines of France, Germany, and the United States are produced from the four noble grapes described in the preceding chapter. However, a number of other European grapes (the *vinifera* varieties) are used in wine making in Europe and the United States. The most important of these are described in this chapter. Some of the wines they make are truly distinguished, and you will find many of their names on wine labels. They are listed alphabetically, first the reds and then the whites.

Alicante Bouschet
This grape is mentioned only because it has red juice—both the pulp and juice are crimson red. A hybrid created to produce alcoholic bulk wines, it was widely planted in California. During Prohibition, it was a favorite with home winemakers because it had plenty of sugar with which to work and it gave magnificently colored wines. It is used now mostly for red generic wines, but it makes a wine worth tasting as a varietal. We enjoyed one bottled by Papagni.

Barbera
This is a red wine grape of the Italian Piedmont and of California. In northwestern Italy the grape produces a dark purple, flavorful wine. With plenty of tannin, it makes the perfect foil for rich Italian food.

In California these grapes produce wines with fullness and body that, for our taste, surpass those Italian vintages with which we are familiar. At the Red Hen Restaurant in Napa Valley, a marvelous tomato-sauced pasta was accompanied by Louis Martini's Barbera, and the wine was the perfect accompaniment for rich, highly seasoned food. Among others making a desirable Barbera wine, besides Martini, are Heitz and Sebastiani.

Carignan

Probably a native of Spain, this grape has spread to France, North Africa, and California. It is the most widely planted wine grape in France, where it is the major ingredient of the French *vin ordinaire*. The wines it produces are variously termed "satisfactory," "ordinary," or "dull."

Carignane also covers a huge acreage in California (note it is spelled with an e in America) and serves as an important blending source in our generic red wines, our *vin ordinaire*. Blended with a bit of Petite Sirah, Zinfandel, and Grenache, it is not a special wine, but it is a great deal better than the French *vin ordinaire*.

In California it is occasionally vinified and bottled as a varietal wine. Try a bottle by Fetzer or Parducci to know the taste.

Gamay

It is always a pleasure to watch a group of Frenchmen come to a decision over a *carte de vin*. Often they will choose a Beaujolais, but only after first surveying the Burgundies and Bordeaux to establish their credentials as experts.

The Gamay grape is the variety responsible for Beaujolais wine. The Beaujolais area is a forty-five-mile strip of granite hills just south of Pouilly-Fuisse in the Burgundy region. The grape is outlawed in the rest of Burgundy as producing wine of little merit, but in Beaujolais, it makes light, beautiful, uncomplicated wines with surging aroma, which are meant to be drunk exuberantly. The young wines are bluish reddish purple with just enough alcohol to keep them for a year or two.

Sad to say, the Gamay grape loses something outside the granite hills of Beaujolais. The Napa Gamay grape of California may be the Gamay of France—there is controversy about that—but the wines it produces rarely equal French Beaujolais.

The Beaujolais vineyards are owned by small farmers who sell through *negociants* (blenders and shippers). There are nine villages whose wines are classified *grands crus*: Fleurie, Moulin-a-Vent, Brouilly, Cote de Brouilly, St. Amour, Morgon, Julienas, Chiroubles, Chenas. The wine of each of these areas is thought to possess individuality, and the colors, tastes, richness, and life span of each are different. Any one of these names on a bottle is some practical assurance of quality. The remaining wines of the region are classified largely on the basis of alcoholic content: Beaujolais-Villages, Beaujolais Superior, and just plain Beaujolais.

Some of the Beaujolais production has been prostituted, in our opinion, to the Nouveau Beaujolais, a pale, skinny, big-nosed wine with a life expectancy of about six months. There is a cult that springs up in November to worship this puny stuff. It is rushed by plane to awaiting audiences as a romantic gesture. The audiences apparently do not know or have forgotten the pleasure of a true Beaujolais.

Gamay Beaujolais

The Gamay Beaujolais is not the Gamay grape of the Beaujolais; it is one of the clones or genetic variants of the Pinot Noir. This darkly pigmented, winey, tart grape grows vigorously in California and for years was mistaken for the grape of the Beaujolais wines. Not so. (For an interesting account of the confusion see Leon D. Adams's *The Wines of America,* pp. 561-62.) However, the Gamay Beaujolais *is* planted in the Beaujolais area of France, and it seems probable that many of the superior qualities of the *grands crus* Beaujolais are the result of its mixture with the darker and longer lasting wines from Gamay Beaujolais.

In California this grape is grown separately to produce a varietal wine, a fresh, fruity, young Pinot Noir. It can be pleasant, but neither the Napa Gamay nor the Gamay Beaujolais makes wines in California that equal the Beaujolais of Burgundy.

Grenache

Grenache is a vigorous, heavy-bearing vine that made its way from Spain to Algeria across southern France and on to California. Depending on district and vinification, it is varyingly noted for red wines, rosé wines, and fortified wines. The berries are sweet; the wines are alcoholic, with a distinctive and lovely bouquet. For a purple red grape, its wines are somewhat lacking in color, a deficiency usually remedied by blending with a more highly pigmented variety. It does make truly beautiful rosé wines, and in the Tavel region of the Rhone and in northern California, it is noted for delicious, refreshing, picnic type wines. The enchanting pink with a hint of orange is most inviting.

The Grenache is chiefly a blending wine. It tempers the wines of Chateauneuf-du-Pape and Cotes du Rhone. Many French "country wines" owe much to the Grenache grape.

In California it has the ability to thrive where most wine grapes broil in the sun. It is planted over wide areas and, as in France, is essential to the rivers of generic red table wines that flow down American throats. In these wines it appears incognito; in the beautiful luncheon rosés it is almost a solo performer.

If you feel a wave of Frenchness coming on, try rosé bottlings by Chapoutier or Delas Freres. If you want a California wine, there are nice varietal bottlings by, among others, Stone Creek.

Lambrusco

Widely grown in northern Italy this grape produces the most popular — but by no means the best — Italian wine imported into the United States. The wine is usually sweet and slightly sparkling, with an unusual aroma that appeals to many wine buyers. Among the favorite brands in this country are Riunite and Cella.

Do not confuse this grape variety with the American species, *Vitis labrusca*.

Malbec

This red grape is one of the lesser contributions to the wines of Bordeaux. It makes lighter and earlier-maturing wines than the Cabernet Sauvignon. The balanced wines have breeding, and many of the Bordeaux reds are improved by the addition of small amounts of Malbec.

The grape is also grown in the neighborhood of Cahors in France and is the principal ingredient of the fine, distinctive wines from that area.

Mission

This extremely productive vine was probably the first European variety to reach California. Its place in the literature of oenology is safely assured in the "department of romance," but its position as a producer of useful wines is the subject of some debate.

Traveling from Spain to Mexico to Baja California and then to coastal California, the Mission grape was carried along the Camino Real by the Franciscan monks. Brought to the San Diego area by Father Junipero Serra, it spread to the missions up the coast. It produced the sacramental wines and the table wines as well. Each mission had its plot of vines. The variety, which never made truly great wine, did not prosper in the more northerly reaches, and later other *vinifera* grapes were used to make much better wines.

Wines from Mission grapes are lush with sugar but poor in color and low in the acidity that is so vital to making a decent wine. Currently the wine is used primarily for blending to make Angelica, honey-sweet and fortified.

In the words of Frank Schoonmaker in *Encyclopedia of Wine* (p. 13): "Angelica [is] one of the poorest and cheapest of American fortified wines, often little more than a blend of sweet, white grape juice and high-proof brandy. It is said to take its name from the city of Los Angeles; if so, it is something of which Los Angeles has no reason to feel proud."

By and large, this is probably true. And yet we remember a lovely dinner in the home of the late Joseph Concannon. The Concannon winery in the Livermore Valley has been producing sacramental and other wines since the late 1800s. After luscious strawberries and cream, Mr. Concannon produced a bottle of 1924 Angelica, discovered some years before when one of their buildings was razed. A deep clear amber, the wine poured like glycerine and "legs" ran up the sides of glasses like rockets. The bouquet was almost lickerish, filled with a bit of depravity one would not expect from a Mission grape. The taste was like an elegant, smooth, and great old white port or Muscat de Frontignan.

Nebbiolo

One of the world's great wine grapes, this is the preeminent red wine grape of Italy. The wines from this fog-loving variety reach their heights in the northwestern Piedmont and Lombardy districts. They are robust and extremely tannic, but after aging in barrel and bottle, marvelously smooth, full, alcoholic wines emerge. Among these are the following:

BAROLO. Italy's best red wine. Deep-colored and slow maturing, it brings to mind those big, full, masculine wines of the Rhone Valley. A deep, long-lived wine, it occasionally rises to extraordinary heights.

BARBARESCO. A neighbor of Barolo, but a lighter, quick-maturing and shorter-lived wine. After a year or two in the bottle, the wine develops a light brownish cast that is termed *onionskin*. A subtle wine, it may exhibit considerable class.

GATTINARA. A wine not frequently encountered, which is a pity. Its production is small. The wine itself is elegant and full bodied, with great bouquet and long life. A big wine!

GHEMME. Another Nebbiolo wine of considerable finesse, reminding one of a Bordeaux wine. It is a cut above the usual image of an Italian red wine.

LESSONA. Much like Ghemme, a lighter wine usually subject to some blending.

VALTELLINA. These wines are from a district away from the Piedmont and bordering on Switzerland. Much deeper in color than most of the other Nebbiolo wines, they are reddish black. Sturdy, tannic, and unpalatable when young, they mature into one of Italy's best red wines and are particularly appreciated by the Swiss. You may well taste your first Valtellina in Switzerland.

The Nebbiolo grape has scant past or future in California. There is little suitable terrain for it. More important, the Italians can put these wines on our shelves at considerably less expense than we could—if we could produce them.

San Gioveto or Sangiovese

This is the major contribution to Chianti wines, in which it is blended with Canaiolo and white Trebbiano. Although some

Chianti can be mediocre or worse, at its best it is a most appetizing red wine. Refreshing, inexpensive, and available, it is a delightful accompaniment to many Italian foods.

The best Chianti, much of it labeled *Chianti Classico,* now comes in high-shouldered Bordeaux bottles rather than the traditional straw-covered bottles. These wines are definitely superior and age well. The bottles often, but not always, carry a seal showing a black cockerel on a red target.

Imitations of Chianti have been produced almost wherever grapes are grown, including California. Rarely made from the Italian varieties of grapes, they have nothing in common with genuine Chianti save the color, but many of them are nevertheless excellent red table wines. We believe in this case it is better to have a well-made imitation than a poor original.

Syrah and Petite Sirah

This grape is a conundrum; mention of Syrah can start an argument. Are we talking about the Rhone Valley Syrah, the California Petite Sirah, or the Duriff grape of France? There is a vast shifting of opinion regarding these grapes. We have neither the space nor the desire to enter into the squabble, and we doubt that you have the patience for it. Therefore, let us say dogmatically that the original Syrah of the Rhone Valley is rarely grown in California, and that the Petite Sirah of California is actually the French Duriff grape that makes a minor contribution along the Rhone River.

Legend has it that returning Crusaders brought the Shiraz grape from Persia. One crusader, by apocryphal account, weary of pillage and plague, set up housekeeping as a holy hermit on the crest of a high bluff on the east bank of the Rhone. Here he set about to right himself with God, grow grapes, and make a bit of wine to ward winter's chill from his liver. On this holy site overlooking the sinuous valley of the Rhone far below, there now exists a tiny *chapelle*. The very footings of the little church lie enshrouded in Syrah vines, which fall away to end at the diluvian plain in the mists below. These are the grapes of Hermitage, probably the best-known of the wines made along the Rhone Valley.

The heavily pigmented, late-ripening berries of the Syrah produce purplish black, inky wines heavy with tannin. These huge, robust wines are too tannic to be drunk young. If cellared until enjoyable, one may still find opaque color, a spicy nose, a mouth filled with pepper, tannin, and a hot, alcoholic finish, but little fruit. There seems to be a hole in the middle.

Certainly the prince of Rhone wines is Cote Rotie—a huge, dark wine from the "roasted slope." Lying along a south-facing curve of the Rhone, not far below Vienne, it is probably the most precipitous vineyard in France. Not 2 miles long and less than 150 acres total area, the curving bank is terraced so steeply as to require stone walls between rows of vines. Any form of mechanized viticulture is impossible, and these hard-won wines are of increasing rarity. An added problem is that this almost impossible vineyard is divided into more than 50 parcels.

The grape is the Syrah, but the robust, enormous wines are softened by up to 20 percent of white wine from the Viognier grape. At their best, these wines are favorites of ours, but one must choose carefully among the various shippers. The wines are in ever greater demand, and there is a sad tendency to "stretch" some of them— leading to thinner wines that become old before they are adolescent.

Should you stop at the Pyramide in Vienne, considered by many of an earlier generation as the greatest restaurant in France, and leave the choice of the red wine to the sommelier, the chances are two to one you will be rewarded with a magnificent, unforgettable Cote Rotie.

In the lower end of the Rhone Valley near Avignon, the home of the popes for forty years, is the land of Chateauneuf-du-Pape. This sturdy, brawny wine is made from the Syrah grape, blended with about a dozen other varieties. The wines are crimson, fullbodied, and alcoholic. They are ready to be drunk after three years but will usually improve with several more years of aging. The best of them are estate bottled, but the district produces volumes of sound lesser wines.

Red wines from the Rhone Valley labeled simply Cotes-duRhone are rough, highly colored, and alcoholic, but the best may make a reasonable substitution for high-priced Bordeaux and Burgundy wines.

In California there is a different story. Without filing a legal brief in support, the Petite Sirah grape is probably the French Duriff, given a new lease on life by California's hospitable climate. Because of its color and tannin, this has always been a useful blending variety. During more difficult times for wine lovers, this color-ful, thick-skinned grape was highly desirable because it withstood shipment to home winemakers.

In 1965 the Concannon Vineyard in Livermore Valley bottled a Petite Sirah varietal wine. It was said to have been made from the "true" Syrah grape. At about this same time a whole gaggle of new wineries were being built and new vineyards planted. Petite Sirah became a vogue, and the biggest, blackest, heaviest wines contested for the new market.

The Petite Sirah in California makes a huge brawling, roustabout wine, an excess of brawn and a dearth of elegance. High in alcohol and all those good things usually called extracts, most of these wines contain little fruit, and merely being big wines may not be enough to maintain a clientele. They seem no longer as fashion-able as they once were, and the winds that brought them to prom-inence may now be blowing out.

The greatest role of these massive wines is in blending. They lend color, alcohol, and tannin to most California Burgundies. Even the lovely rose tint in Paul Masson's Pink Champagne is the result of 2 to 3 percent of Petite Sirah. Burgess Cellars made an outstanding varietal wine from Petite Sirah, but discontinued it in 1978. Among others making a varietal are Freemark Abbey, Gemello, Robert Mondavi, Parducci, and Ridge.

Joseph Phelps makes a varietal wine using the true French Syrah grape. It differs from the Petite Sirah (Duriff) but, in our opinion, is not substantially better.

Zinfandel

This dark, heavy-producing grape is California's gift to the world of wine. Probably the most widely planted red grape in California, this *vinifera* variety had no known European origin un-til 1967 when a United States plant pathologist found an apparently identical grape growing in the heel of Italy.

In California these unique dark wines have been enjoyed since the Civil War, but for decades they were used chiefly in blending and extending other wines. To this day they are usually a major component of California wines labeled Burgundy. They add per-fume, color, and enchanting flavor to some otherwise dull vintages. In the last twenty years, however, Zinfandel has made one of

California's outstanding varietal wines, and it is highly recommended in this form.

The wines are deeply colored. At their best they have a "bramble" nose, a "bramble" taste, and a great bouquet — almost a canopy — of blackberry. The flavor of berries and spice is full and heavy in the mouth. There is no mistaking this for any other wine.

The Zinfandel grape, however, is as multifaceted as Chardonnay. It is successfully vinified in a number of styles. Callaway and Montevina, for example, turn it into enormously powerful, jammy wines, which seem a pure extract of berries. Ridge makes a plethora of wines of intense flavor. Clos du Val vinifies the Zinfandel in the manner of a lovely Bordeaux. Mount Veeder and Joseph Phelps make wines filled with brambles, but brambles that somehow react with finesse. Zinfandel Blancs (white wines) are made, as are Zinfandel rosés and Nouveau Zinfandels. There is a bottle for every purse, and one to be drunk with almost any meat. But a word of warning: As Zinfandels age they rapidly lose their characteristic and delightful fruit. After ten years you may find they have become a sort of modified Cabernet Sauvignon, without true greatness. Zinfandels are most enjoyable as young, lusty wines.

In southern Italy this grape is known as Primitivo di Gioia. The heavy-bodied wines produced there are blended and not bottled under the grape name.

The foregoing list covers the major red varieties of the European grapes. The list following covers the major white varieties, in addition to the Chardonnay and Riesling described in Chapter 4.

Aligote

At one time this variety was an important part of the Burgundian scene, but it long since has been banished to the back room. Growing on the back side of the Burgundian slope and here and there with the Gamay grapes, the Aligote produces an inexpensive white wine: dry, crisp, simple, and with little aftertaste. It is a favorite aperitif wine among Burgundians. It is usually the first wine served at the banquets of the Confrerie des Chevaliers du Tastevin held at the Clos de Vougeot. We have never tasted this wine elsewhere in France, except in blended wines. We have never tasted it as an American varietal wine.

Chenin Blanc

This is the grape of the Loire Valley—a land of the great chateaux, pale blue skies, placid rivers, mushroom caves, orchards, and exquisite freshwater fish. The vines are vigorous, heavy producers, and the greenish yellow grapes are literally filled with rich fruit, high acids, and enough sugar.

Known in France also as the Pineau de la Loire, the grape is vinified in many different ways. It is the only grape used in Vouvrays, both those that are dry, floral, and delicate and those that are richer and sweeter. Occasionally attacked by the beneficent mold *Botrytis cinerea,* the late-picked grapes make wines similar to a Sauternes. True sparkling wines are also made from this grape by the champagne method, and others with just enough remaining fermentation to be *petillant* and put sparkles on your tongue.

There is considerable variation in Loire Chenin Blancs. When you find a particularly good one, remember the name of the *negociant.*

This grape does extremely well in California, especially in the Monterey area, and many lovely varietal Chenin Blancs are now available. They may be as dry as a bone or as succulent as Callaway's Sweet Nancy, a "botrytised" wine.

Mount Veeder's Chenin Blanc is dry, with good alcoholic content, and it will accompany shellfish, sole, and salmon or serve as an aperitif. Among other worthwhile California vintages are those from Burgess, Christian Brothers, Kenwood, Robert Mondavi, Parducci, Sterling, and Yverdon. For those attempting to interest another person in wine, the Christian Brothers Pineau de la Loire may prove a satisfactory springboard.

Columbard

This variety is from the Charente region of France, where it is also known as the Colombar of Pied-Tendre. It is very productive, high in acid, and, together with the Folle Blanche, makes the wines from which cognac is distilled.

Grown over very wide areas in California where it is called French Colombard, this grape produces a pale, fresh, somewhat acid wine with a characteristically flowery nose. It has the sort of bouquet and taste that may make one falsely impute sweetness to a dry wine. Its greatest use in California is as a white blending wine. Its aroma is readily detected in many a California "Chablis" and less expensive sparkling wines. It is here and there available as a varietal wine.

Gewurztraminer

Wines from this white grape are immediately identified by their aromatic bouquet and spicy perfumed taste. They are lovely wines readily distinguished from any other. The grape is a clone of the Traminer grape. The prefix *gewurz* means spicy, and no other grape is more accurately named. It seems most at home in the Alsace region of France, but it does very well in California's cooler microclimates and in Oregon and Washington.

The strong vines yield small berries that have a bronzy blush pink skin when mature. The best wines come from grapes in the cooler regions. Hot days may diminish their characteristic spice and substitute bitterness.

The wine is a clear, lively greenish yellow. There is a tendency towards a little bitterness in the prolonged aftertaste when the fruit and spice have worn away. Some wine lovers think Gewurztraminers too obvious, but we ask why fault a wine that so ably accompanies those heavy sausage, cabbage, and pork dishes that defy any other wine?

There is a West Coast tendency to vinify this variety for a wine less dry than its Alsatian counterpart. These wines still have a reasonable quota of spice, but they tend to be more rounded, soft, with almost gay floral qualities and occasionally a bit of *Botrytis.*

In Alsace the names of Hugel and Trimbach are excellent signposts to good quality. In California Grand Cru vineyards, Hacienda Wine Cellars, Chateau St. Jean, and Joseph Phelps among others produce excellent Gewurztraminers. A particular value for the money is available from Paul Masson.

The California Gewurztraminers are often the wines to accompany menus of Chinese food or curried dishes. They have the acidity of the Gewurztraminer grape and the remnant of sugar to bless strange tastes. While writing this chapter, we had a charcoal-grilled ham steak, fresh succotash, and fresh tomatoes with a vinegar-sugar-oil-basil dressing. A Clos du Bois 1978 Gewurztraminer proved a delightful counterpoint to the supper: deep amber color; viscous "legs"; typical, unforgettable nose; and just enough sugar and acid to blend with the food. This is one of our all-purpose wines — try both American and Alsatian bottlings.

Muller-Thurgau

This white grape, named for the man who developed it, is widely planted in Germany. There has been doubt about its antecedents, but Peter Sichel, an authority on German wines, declares it is a cross of Riesling varieties. Dr. Muller-Thurgau was attempting to retain the elegance and flavor of the Riesling and at the same time increase the yield. His efforts were quite successful. Vinification of the variety results in young, fresh, and fruity wines, which should be enjoyed in their youth. The Muller-Thurgau has not, as yet, found much of a home in America.

Muscadet

Don't confuse this grape with the Muscat. The Muscadet is the grape of the lower Loire Valley in France, and its true name is Melon. On 20,000 acres of vineyards owned in small patches by peasant growers, the grapes are grown to make this unique, tart, fresh wine. The pale wines, most prominently made in the Region de Sevre-et-Maine, are a favorite accompaniment for oysters and shellfish. Dry to a pucker, these wines are in vogue among lovers of seafoods.

Among the many to be considered, we have enjoyed the bottlings of Chateau de Rochefort, Domaine de Beau Site, Louis Beauchant, Marquis de Goulaine, and Domaine de L'Hyverie.

These French wines seem to have no exact counterpart in California.

Muscat

This is a triple-threat grape, as useful for making wine and commercial raisins as for a table grape. We are interested only in the first category. A huge family of grapes, the Muscats have a definite, characteristic bouquet and flavor. Their chief use in this respect is in dessert or fortified wines. The great wines of Sauternes and Barsac contain enough Muscat to perfume the vintage. Along the Mediterranean district of France, the unique fortified wines of Frontignan owe their flavor and nose to the Muscat. In northern Italy the Muscat Canelli is the principal grape in the sweet, sparkling wine, Asti Spumante.

In California the Muscat and its family are chiefly used in blending sweet, aromatic white wines. In varietal form, these grapes make exciting, delicate, low-alcohol white wines. The one coming to mind first is Louis Martini's Muscat Amabile, usually available only at the winery.

It should be noted also that the Muscat of Alexandria grape has been the source of the cheap fortified wines in common usage along America's skid rows. Thus, they have been most commonly associated with the depraved alcoholic. However, if you try one of the more elegant, limited production wines, you may well help divest this wine of its degrading "Muscatel" image. Muscat needs you to regain its social stature.

Pinot Blanc

This is a true Pinot grape, doubtless a nonpigmented genetic variation or clone of the Pinot Noir. For many years this variety was confused and interplanted with the Chardonnay, which is the reason the latter is sometimes incorrectly called Pinot Chardonnay. This intermingling of the two varieties is most prevalent along the Cote d'Or in Burgundy, and many a Meursault and lesser Montrachet may owe a portion of its softness and perfume to the Pinot Blanc. Many of the less expensive white Burgundies may well be mostly Pinot Blanc.

In California the Pinot Blanc's success has been modest up to now for two reasons. First, many of the vines are virus infected, but virus free stocks are now available. Second, in this happy climate the grapes most frequently have been cultivated for quantity rather than quality, with a subsequent diminution of their character.

Very creditable white wines — light, dry, delicate, youthful, with both adequate sugar and acidity — are made from the Pinot Blanc. However, we suspect more of it is used in blends than is bottled under its own name.

This grape, which likes a cool climate, does well in our Northwest and also in Italy, where it is vinified into delightful wines, both still and sparkling.

If you can find a varietal Pinot Blanc, we suggest you taste it vis-à-vis a Chardonnay *and* a less expensive white Burgundy. You may be surprised. Pinot Blanc does not have to be the "poor man's Chardonnay." If the tendency toward a huge crop is thwarted and the resultant rich grapes are vinified as is Chardonnay, few might note the difference. These are attractive, occasionally exciting wines. Look for, among others, Chalone Vineyard, Chateau St. Jean, Monterey Vineyards, Smothers, and Wente Bros. These are wines with real personalities. Test the Smothers wine against a Meursault. There is a substantial price difference, a difference that time may eliminate.

Sauvignon Blanc

This is a classic white grape, running a very close third behind Chardonnay and White Riesling. It is the major grape in the white wines of the Graves district in Bordeaux; it contributes to the great wines in the Sauternes district; it is responsible for delightful wines in the Loire Valley and in cooler climates of California. It is a good grower, producing pale green grapes with rich flavor and characteristic bouquet.

In the aggressive, austere white wines of Graves, the aroma is typical and the sweet-fruitiness is present in the must, but fermentation to dryness deals rather harshly with these generosities and results in firm wines with scant warmth.

Along the upper Loire River the Sauvignon Blanc is the source of the wines of Sancerre and Pouilly-Fume. These famous dry wines are more gentle than their Bordeaux counterparts. There are fewer sharp corners, and the flavors are allowed to flourish with the bouquet. These are fresh, youthful wines that are the natural accompaniment of delicate fish and seafoods. Try a bottle of fairly well-chilled Ladoucette Pouilly-Fume with a grilled Dover sole.

In California the Sauvignon Blanc was almost a catastrophe. Wines made from this grape did not sell, and the plantings were being pulled up to make way for varieties in greater demand. Robert Mondavi saved the variety and put it on the proper path. He blended in 10 percent of Semillon to smooth rough edges and produced a delightfully fresh, young wine, which he called Fume Blanc. (In some parts of the Loire Valley the grape is called Blanc Fume.) Trading a little on the similarity to Pouilly-Fume, this wine won acceptance in the marketplace. Soon it seemed every vintner in California was toying with the variety, and now wine shop shelves are loaded with Fume Blancs and Sauvignon Blancs.

You can enter this lovely world through, among others,

Robert Mondavi Fume Blanc, Callaway Vineyard Fume White Mist, Chateau Ste. Michelle Fume Blanc (a Washington State vintage), Christian Brothers Fume Blanc, Monterey Vineyards Sauvignon Blanc-Botrytis, Joseph Phelps Sauvignon Blanc (85 percent Sauvignon Blanc, 15 percent Semillon), and Dry Creek Fume Blanc. There is now a wide spectrum of wines from this grape in California. Read the labels, pay your money, and take your choice.

One morning at the Montevina Winery a few years ago, Cary Gott, the winemaker, opened a bottle of his 1976 Sauvignon Blanc, and the enormous bouquet diffused immediately through the tasting room. The wine was a splendid giant, about 16 percent alcohol, dramatically intense in both aroma and taste. Here, high in Amador County, the home of Sutter's Creek, the Gold Rush, and great Zinfandels, was the world's largest Sauvignon Blanc. The alcohol was a bit hot in the long aftertaste. Gott said he had the choice of either saving the unusual intensity of the wine or of diluting its alcoholic dimensions and losing some of its effect. He chose to leave it alone — and very wisely, too.

Semillon

This is the luscious white grape of the Sauternes wines. A vigorous grower, the grape is a deep yellow with occasionally blush pink cheeks. Its thin skin makes it an easy target for the *Botrytis cinerea* (in French, *pourriture noble,* or noble rot) that is responsible for the magnificent dessert wines of the Sauternes and Barsac districts of Bordeaux. The gravelly clay soil of the area is what the Semillon requires for its fullest development. Here, as the berries ripen in the warm, humid autumn, the *Botrytis* spores germinate, pierce the tender skins, and the grape loses its water content and collapses on a honey-sweet center, rich in glycerine, sugar, acid, and myriad aromatic compounds. As the little *maitre de chai* (cellar master) at Chateau Coutet said, "The grapes are covered with tiny toadstools."

These wizened, moldy grapes are the source of the most elegant sweet wines in the world. The must has a monumental sugar content. As it ferments to 14 to 17 percent alcohol, yeasts are killed, and the remaining sugar content makes for extraordinary sweet wines with an enormous overlay of fruit and a backbone of considerable acid. The *Botrytis* itself contributes to the honey taste.

Occasionally an alcohol-resistant yeast may turn up. The Chateau Coutet 1916 Barsac is said to have measured 20 percent alcohol. Holding the bottle of dark amber wine in hand, one wondered how it had ever made it through two world wars.

These beautiful Sauternes and Barsacs are brought to their heights by blending with Sauvignon Blanc and a wee bit of Muscadelle for perfume. The Sauvignon furnishes the acid when needed. The single *grand premier cru* of Sauternes is the Chateau d'Yquem. This incomparable gold wine comes from about 220 acres of principally Semillon vines. The wine has not only fruit, creaminess, and finesse, but it also is quite alone in its manifest distinction and breeding.

Other dessert wines in this area are also favorites. We find Chateau Coutet quite distinct in that its higher acidity gives the fruit and sugar the added character of a long racy aftertaste, which maintains itself for an incredible period of time. And among other wines of the district that can be served with pride are Chateau La Tour-Blanche, Chateau Climens, Chateau Rieussec, and Chateau Filhot.

Occasionally there are "off" years, in which the *Botrytis* does not arrive on time, or some meteorologic catastrophe develops and the wines do not reach sufficient sugar content to make a characteristic Sauternes or Barsac. They are then fermented to comparative dryness and sold as Bordeaux Superior. In the case of Chateau d'Yquem, the wine is bottled under a Chateau Y label. These wines are similar to a medium-dry white Graves, but with a little more class and bouquet.

Although the Semillon grape is at its best in the Sauternes district, it also grows well in the Graves area of Bordeaux. Here it contributes about one-third of the blend of the white Graves wines; the other wines used are largely from Sauvignon Blanc. If you enjoy the crisp white Bordeaux wines, most of the fruit and all of the soft roundness can be attributed to the Semillon grapes.

The variety grows well in California, but it is definitely not an individual performer. To date, few Sauternes-type wines are made in California, where very little spontaneous *Botrytis* infection occurs. Several attempts have been made to inoculate the ripening grapes with *Botrytis* spores, but the results have been inconsistent.

However, the Semillon vinified as a distinct dry wine adds roundness and depth in blending. It is not usually made and bottled

4

as a varietal wine. To do so would create a ghost of what might have been.

Sylvaner

This yellow green grape changes to yellow amber under the sun and matures early. It is vigorous and dependable. Usually planted in areas where the Riesling does not do well, it yields wines that are light, fresh, and of casual quality. It makes a soft sweet wine in Germany, where the name is spelled Silvaner, and it also makes a dry, acidic wine in Alsace. It is sometimes called Franken or, erroneously, Franken Riesling.

In California the Sylvaner makes a pleasant sort of wine, often blended with the more aristocratic Riesling. As a varietal wine it has been somewhat disappointing. However, try a Monterey Vineyard bottling; it has a growing reputation and clientele.

California Hybrids

Some fascinating new grapes are showing up over our vinous horizon. Dr. Harold Olmo of the University of California at Davis has worked on the production of the new *vinifera* varieties since the early 1930s. One of them, the Emerald Riesling, has already achieved considerable commercial success and acceptance by wine lovers. These new varieties were developed either to overcome certain cultural difficulties or to combine the most desirable characteristics of several grapes. Among these are Ruby Cabernet, Carmine, Carnelian, and Flora. There are others. Although not such a hybrid, the Pinot St. George was identified by Dr. Olmo in a vineyard of unknown ancestry. This grape is now vinified by Christian Brothers into one of their outstanding red wines.

These California hybrids may well serve to produce some of the collector's items of tomorrow.

It is not possible in a book of this scope to cover every European grape. We have listed the ones responsible for the wines you are most likely to encounter in an American wine shop. We have omitted a number: the grapes grown in Spain from which the red Rioja table wines are made; the grapes of Portugal that produce the popular rosés Lancers and Mateus; the grapes of Greece that make Retsina, a wine strongly flavored with resin.

If you search as you travel about the country, you may find wines from Sicily, Rumania, Bulgaria, Yugoslavia, Russia, Israel, England, South Africa, New Zealand, Australia, Chile, Argentina, and Algeria. When you find them, try them. Some may please you very much. But buy a single bottle the first time!

6. Grapes – the Americans

T H E first white settlers on the Atlantic seaboard made wines from the native American grapes and were disappointed with the results. They then attempted to grow the European grapes, but all of the imported vines died, unable to survive the cold winters and the attacks of plant pests and diseases to which the native vines were immune. It was not until decades later when *vinifera* vines were brought to New Mexico and California that European grapes were grown successfully in America.

Leon D. Adams, the widely known authority on wine, has an interesting theory that the United States would never have adopted the Prohibition Amendment if the early settlers had succeeded in making good wine. In his authoritative book *The Wines of America* (p. 20) he writes: "Without good wine as a moderate daily beverage, the colonists and their descendants drank hard apple cider, then applejack and rum, and finally adopted whiskey as the national drink."

Despite their first unsuccessful efforts, the colonists persisted in their attempts to domesticate the wild American grapes and produce acceptable wine from them. By the latter part of the eighteenth century and the first years of the nineteenth, commercial wineries were established in several eastern seaboard states. Today, after a long series of ups and downs, successful vineyards and wineries are operating in many states east of the Mississippi, particularly in New York State.

Most of the grape varieties native to America belong to the

species *Vitis labrusca.* Some belong to *Vitis rotundifolia.* (Do not confuse *labrusca,* the American grape species, with Lambrusco, a grape variety belonging to the *vinifera* species and widely grown in Italy.)

There is a distinct, quickly recognizable difference in wines made from the European *vinifera* grapes and wine produced entirely from the American *labrusca* varieties. Most of the *labrusca* wines have a grapelike flavor, somewhat characteristic of old-fashioned Concord grape juice and usually referred to as "foxy." There would seem to be little connection between a fox and the flavor of grapes, but the wine writer Bern C. Ramey says in his book *The Great Wine Grapes and the Wines They Make* that foxy probably came from Aesop's fable "The Fox and the Grapes." Whatever its origin, foxy is a term resented by many eastern winemakers and by persons who enjoy the flavor of grapes in their wine.

For many years eastern winemakers worked solely with the American grapes, but they now also use hybrid grapes, blurring the distinction between eastern and western wines. The hybrids are produced by crossing *labrusca* and *vinifera* varieties to combine the sturdiness of the *labrusca* vines in the eastern climate with more of the flavor of the *vinifera* grapes. In recent years some eastern vineyards, by improved cultivation methods, have also been growing *vinifera* varieties and making wine from them.

With this brief explanation of a subject that could easily fill a book, here is a list of some of the grapes used in wine making in the United States east of the Mississippi River. Most of the wines, but not all, are sold under the name of the grape.

Aurora

One of the hybrid grapes developed in France by crossing *labrusca* and *vinifera* varieties. It produces a rather sweet, fragrant, white table wine of good quality but not particularly distinctive taste. It is sometimes labeled Sauterne, although it does not resemble a French Sauternes. It is also used to make sparkling wine.

Baco Noir

One of the most successful hybrids. It produces a red table

wine with a distinctive flavor, somewhat resembling Cabernet Sauvignon if it is properly aged.

Catawba

A native grape that was a favorite in American wine making for many years. It is used to make both still and sparkling red, white, and rosé wines, mostly sweet and quite grapy. It was the most popular wine grape in the United States in the middle of the last century, and Ohio, where it was extensively grown, was the leading state in the country in wine production. Ohio now ranks well below California and New York.

Chelois

A French hybrid that produces a light, red, fruity table wine with some hint of its *labrusca* ancestry, which tends to disappear with age.

Concord

The most widely planted grape in the eastern United States today. It is the primary ingredient for most grape juice and jelly, but it is also used to produce sweet kosher wines, eastern port and Burgundy, and cold duck. Most wine experts consider the juice and the jelly far superior to the wine.

De Chaunac

A French hybrid that produces a good, red table wine, particularly when aged. The wine is dark colored and rich.

Delaware

Considered the best of the American wine grapes by most wine experts, Delaware, unlike many other American varieties, has good sugar content. Widely planted throughout the eastern United States, it produces both red and white soft, fruity table wines. The white is probably the best white table wine made in the eastern United States, with the possible exception of wines from some of the newer hybrids. It is also used in champagne. Some students think there may be a touch of *vinifera* in its ancestry, a possibility in some of the other so-called native vines, too, but no one knows for sure.

Dutchess

A white grape once widely planted in eastern vineyards, but now less so because it is difficult to grow. It makes a pleasing wine without the grapy flavor of many eastern grapes.

Niagara

A popular native grape that produces both dry and sweet wines, pleasant but without distinctive flavor.

Scuppernong

A grape with a highly distinctive flavor unlike any other, it grows only in the southeastern region of the United States. It belongs to the *rotundifolia* species and is also known as the Muscadine. The vines are enormous and spreading; a single vine may cover an acre. The bronzy green berries grow in small clusters like cherry tomatoes. Dating back to the mid-sixteenth century in Florida, Scuppernong wine was probably the first native wine produced in America, and it is still popular. The wine is amber, somewhat bitter, with almost too much taste. If sweetened, as it usually is, it takes on a plumy, musky nose, which will hide even the foxy taste of Concord wines. The original Virginia Dare, which was highly popular in the early days of this century, was a blend of Scuppernong and Concord. Virginia Dare, with a different blend, is still popular today, and Mother Vineyard Scuppernong is one of the best-selling wines in America.

Seyval Blanc

This French hybrid produces a very good, clean-tasting, crisp white wine, which is somewhat reminiscent of Chardonnay.

7. How to Read a Label

 I F you can't judge a book by its cover, as we are often told, can you judge a wine by its label? No, but if you know how to read a label, you can tell what *should* be in the bottle. Labels can be both attractive and confusing. A friend reports he took a walk in downtown Tokyo one evening shortly after arriving in that city and found the streets ablaze with neon signs. It was a dazzling display, beautiful in a way, he said, but also somewhat disquieting. He was surrounded by information and had no idea what any of it meant. A novice in a wine shop might feel the same way, but learning to read wine labels is much easier than learning Japanese.

A label usually will provide at least four clues to the wine. It will identify the general type of wine, sometimes naming the grape from which it was made. It will report where the wine was made and who made it. Usually it will indicate the year in which it was made. You can find most of this quickly on almost all wine labels, but the method of presenting the information differs from country to country, not because of language but because laws and customs vary. France and Germany, for example, have stricter laws governing wine production and labeling than the United States, and their labels are, therefore, more informative.

United States Labels

American labels identify the type of wine in one of two ways: by naming the grape variety primarily used in making it (e.g.,

Cabernet Sauvignon) or by identifying it as a general type of wine (e.g., Burgundy or champagne). The former is called a varietal wine, and the latter, a generic wine.

Under U.S. regulations a varietal wine must contain not less than 75 percent of the grape named; so if you buy an American wine labeled Cabernet Sauvignon, you know that it should have the aroma and taste typical of that grape. Before 1983 the minimum requirement was 51 percent. The grape varieties you are most likely to see on American labels are described in the preceding chapters.

Most generic labels, sometimes called semigeneric, use names borrowed from famous European wine-producing regions, and a generic label implies that the wine is similar to wine produced in the region from which it takes its name. The similarity may be close, or it may be nonexistent.

Generic labels used most frequently in the United States are Burgundy, Chablis, champagne, Sauterne, Rhine, Chianti, sherry, and port. The first four are famous wine areas of France. Rhine is borrowed from the famous river valley in Germany, Chianti from Italy, sherry from Spain, and port from the great dessert wine made in Portugal.

The generic label does not mean that the American wine is made from the same grape as its presumed European relative. In France the great red Burgundies are made from the Pinot Noir grape, but in America wines labeled Burgundy may be made from any grape, often Carignane, Zinfandel, and Petite Sirah. In France Chablis is made only from the Chardonnay grape; in America Chablis can be any white wine. Sauternes (always spelled with a final *s* in France) is made from the Semillon and Sauvignon Blanc grapes in France and is always sweet. In America it may be either sweet or dry. To be labeled champagne, an American wine must be made in the same general manner as French champagne, but there is no restriction here on the grapes that may be used as there is in France. Some American champagne resembles the French product in taste; much of it does not. If the label says the wine was fermented in "this" bottle, the quality is likely to be good.

In Germany the best Rhine wines are made from the Riesling and Muller-Thurgau grapes; in the United States any white table wine may be labeled Rhine. In Europe sherry is the fortified wine made by a complex process in Spain. Some American-made sherries closely resemble the Spanish product; others do not. In Europe port is a sweet, fortified dessert wine made in Portugal. As with sherry, American-labeled port may be similar to the original, or it may be completely different and vastly inferior. Portuguese regulations require that all port wine shipped to the United States from Portugal be labeled Porto.

There are good American generic wines, but it is best to ignore the European connotations on their labels and judge them on their own merits. If you find an American Chablis you like, enjoy it. If you want an American wine that resembles French Chablis, you are more likely to find it in a varietal wine labeled Chardonnay. If you are seeking the American equivalent of a German Rhine wine, try one labeled White Riesling or Johannisberg Riesling.

European connotations can be not only irrelevant but quite confusing. An example is an American wine labeled St. Emilion (White Burgundy). St. Emilion is a wine district in the Bordeaux, not Burgundy, region of France. St. Emilion is also the name of a grape, but it is not used on a French label for white wine. St. Emilion may be a pleasant American wine, but it has no relationship to either a French St. Emilion or a French white Burgundy.

The use of European names on American wines was not born of deception. When the wine industry began to develop in this country, most wine drinkers were familiar only with the wine names of Europe. There were few restrictions covering labels, and winemakers used whatever European names they thought their wine most closely resembled. Many of the first vineyards were established by persons who were first or second generation immigrants and their hope was to duplicate here the wines of Europe.

As competition increased and the wine-drinking public became more discriminating, winemakers sought more specific labels. Frank Schoonmaker, joined later by Alexis Lichine, urged California vintners to use varietal labels. Simultaneously some winemakers began to concentrate not on imitating European wines but on producing the best wine possible from grapes that would thrive in American soils and climates. If a winemaker produced a superior wine from the Pinot Noir grape, labeling it Pinot Noir would distinguish it from American Burgundies, which could be made from less costly grapes. Similarly, an American white wine made from the Chardonnay grape would be more distinctively labeled as a Chardonnay than as a Chablis, which in the United States could be anything (even pink!).

1976 Ⓐ

Monteviña ⒷꞮ

Sauvignon Blanc ©
Amador County Ⓓ

Grown, Produced & Bottled by Monteviña Wines
Shenandoah Valley, Plymouth, California

ALCOHOL 15.7% BY VOLUME

ESTATE BOTTLED Ⓔ

AMERICAN LABEL

Ⓐ   *Year grapes were harvested*
Ⓑ   *Winery*
©   *Varietal wine made primarily from Sauvignon Blanc*
     grapes
Ⓓ   *75 percent or more of grapes came from this county*
Ⓔ   *Grapes were grown and wine fermented and bottled*
     by winery

Varietal wines are usually more expensive to produce than are generics. The White (or Johannisberg) Riesling grape, for example, produces wine of high quality but produces less of it for the effort involved than some other white wine grapes. The vintner who makes a White Riesling wine, therefore, is justified in charging more for it than for a wine labeled simply Rhine wine or Riesling, either of which can be made in the United States with other grapes.

Although in general the higher quality American wines carry varietal labels, this does not mean that generic wines are poor wines. They may be excellent values for the price.

A few generic labels describe the wine in direct terms instead of using European geographic names, for example, rosé, red table wine, sparkling wine, and so on. A few wines are labeled with names that are neither varietal nor generic. These proprietary wines have names chosen by their makers, for example, Paul Masson's Emerald Dry, Fetzer's Mountain Red, and Boordy's Boordyblumchen.

The American label will report what vineyard or winery made the wine. You will find this a fairly reliable guide to quality. There are differences in a vineyard's wines from year to year, but if you like a certain Chenin Blanc this year, it is likely you will find it good next year, too. Most vintners try to be consistent in the quality they produce from year to year.

The label may also show the name of a viticultural area, for example, Alexander Valley. If so, U.S. regulations effective in 1983 provide that 85 percent of the grapes used in the wine must come from the area and the area must be an officially approved region with geographic features that give its wines distinctive qualities. If the label carries a date, 95 percent of the grapes must come from the stated year. California regulations require that a wine identified as coming from that state must be made 100 percent from California grapes. New York State regulations require that 75 percent of a New York State wine be from grapes grown in the state.

The words *estate-bottled* mean that, under 1983 regulations, the wine was made and bottled on the vineyard's premises from grapes grown in its fields within one viticultural area. An estate-bottled label does not guarantee a superior wine, but it usually indicates the vineyard has set high standards and, by controlling the entire process from cultivation to bottling, is attempting to make a superior product.

Some American labels show the vintage; others do not. In its most common use, *vintage* means simply the year the grapes were harvested. It does not imply, except with two types of wine, that the wine is superior. Every wine is a vintage wine unless it is a blend of grapes grown in different years. The exceptions are Portuguese porto and French champagne, which are usually blends of several years and show no year or vintage on the label. In an exceptional year when a superior wine is made without blending wines from other years, the year is printed on the label, and the wine is known as a vintage porto or a vintage champagne.

In France and Germany the quality of the grape harvest varies sharply from year to year because of the wide variations in weather, and the date is significant in judging the wine. It is often said that there is no need for a date on American wines because the weather in the United States wine regions is more consistent from year to year, which results in wines of even quality. This is partly true. American grape growers rarely have the climate disasters that sometimes occur in Europe, but there are differences in grape quality from year to year.

A date is helpful for another reason. It tells you the age of the wine. Some wines improve with age — Cabernet Sauvignon and Chardonnay, for example — and others should be drunk young. Most ordinary white wines lose their freshness if they are kept long in the bottle.

Some American wines are labeled nonvintage, or NV, which means that wines of two or more years have been blended. This marking is more likely on *vin ordinaire* than on superior wines, but this does not mean the wine isn't worth the selling price.

French Labels

The French pattern of grape growing and wine making is different from the American, and so are French labeling regulations. In the United States most wineries produce several different kinds of wine. It is not unusual for a winery to offer as many as six or eight. The French, having learned from centuries of experience where various grapes will produce the best wines, tend to concentrate on producing one or two types in each region.

Reflecting this, the French labeling system for better wines is based on two assumptions: (1) that the best way to identify a wine is to indicate where it originated geographically, and (2) that the best way to protect the reputations of the individual regions is through strict regulations on winemakers who use the geographical designations on their labels. Thus, when a French label reports where a wine was made, it is also reporting what type of wine it is and what grapes were used to make it.

Most of the French wines you are likely to encounter in this country will have the words *appellation controlee* printed on the label along with the name of an area or place. This means that the use of that name is controlled by official regulations. It is a guarantee that the wine was made in the named area from specified grapes that were cultivated, harvested, and fermented in a prescribed manner. The controlled name may be a large wine region or a district within that region or a village within the district or even a single vineyard or chateau.

The smaller or more specific the area named on the label, the stricter the regulations on growing the grapes and making the wine. To illustrate, Bordeaux is one of the great wine regions of France and of the world. The Medoc is a district within the Bordeaux region. To be entitled to the Medoc label, a wine has to meet stricter standards than one labeled Bordeaux. It usually will command a higher price. Within the Medoc are communes with *appellation controlee* names, and within the communes are individual chateaux or vineyards with controlled names. A wine bearing the name of a chateau — for example, Chateau Beychevelle in the St. Julien commune — will have met even stricter standards and will carry an even higher price. For obvious reasons winemakers will use the most specific *appellation controlee* label for which they can qualify.

Regulations vary widely from area to area, designed in each case to produce the best wine grape and the best wine of which the area is capable. In general, this means that the more specific the *appellation controlee* label the better the wine, although this is not a certainty. The vagaries of weather and the carelessness of vintners can distort the most carefully planned results.

There are hundreds of *appellation controlee* designations. Only a wine scholar is familiar with all of them, but a knowledge of the general characteristics of the major wine regions and the grapes grown in each will provide an introduction to French labels and French wines. The major regions are Bordeaux, Burgundy, Champagne, Alsace, the Loire Valley, and the Rhone Valley.

MIS ᴇɴ BOUTEILLE ᴀᴜ CHATEAU Ⓐ

GRAND VIN
DE
CHATEAU LATOUR Ⓑ

PREMIER GRAND CRU CLASSE Ⓒ

1966 Ⓓ

DÉPOSÉ

APPELLATION PAUILLAC CONTROLEE Ⓔ

FRENCH LABEL

- Ⓐ *Estate bottled*
- Ⓑ *World famous winery*
- Ⓒ *Officially classified as a first growth, highest ranking of the Medoc district*
- Ⓓ *Year grapes were harvested*
- Ⓔ *Wine has met quality standards required in Pauillac commune*

BORDEAUX. The region in southwest France surrounding the city of that name. Its best red and white wines are among the finest in the world. Within the Bordeaux region are five districts: Medoc (including the communes of Margaux, Moulis, St. Julien, Pauillac, and St. Estephe); Graves; Sauternes (including Barsac); St. Emilion; and Pomerol.

The best wines of these districts will be labeled with the name of the district or, if made under more rigid controls, the name of a village, commune, or chateau. Medoc, St. Emilion, and Pomerol are famous for their red wines; Graves for both red and white; and Sauternes for its rich sweet white wine. The red wine grapes permitted in Bordeaux *appellation controlee* wines are chiefly Cabernet Sauvignon, Cabernet Franc, and Merlot, with smaller amounts of several others. The primary white wine grapes are Semillon and Sauvignon Blanc.

Wine made and bottled at the vineyard where the grapes were grown will be so labeled. The term usually is *mise en bouteilles au domaine* or *mise au chateau*. If a *negociant*, or shipper, purchased the wines from the vineyards and completed the process of aging and bottling, the label will carry that name.

In many of the French wine districts, official classifications have been made, and references to *crus,* or growths, appear on labels of those vineyards, ranking the vineyards according to quality. For example, a St. Emilion vineyard classified in the highest quality category is in the *premier grand cru classe* (first great growth). The classification lists are long and detailed. They are printed in a number of wine books available at your library or book store.

BURGUNDY. The wine region southeast of Paris that makes a very small amount of the world's finest red and white wines. The major districts within the region are Cote d'Or, Chablis, Beaujolais, Maconnais, and Chalonnais. As in Bordeaux, within each district are villages or communes and vineyards whose names are controlled for labeling purposes under the *appellation controlee* regulations. Unlike in Bordeaux, most vineyards in Burgundy have many owners, each controlling only a small portion. Much Burgundy wine, therefore, is bottled by *negociants* or shippers who buy wines from various growers in the same vineyard and blend them and label them with the vineyard name. The label will note this, and the name of the *negociant* or shipper can be a reliable indication of the quality of the wine.

The great red and white Burgundies come from the Cote d'Or. Only the Pinot Noir grape is used in the reds, and only the Chardonnay may be used in the renowned whites, the most celebrated of which come from the Montrachet vineyard and its immediate neighbors.

Chablis, a rare and excellent white wine, comes from a small district in Burgundy around the town of the same name. All Chablis is made from the Chardonnay grape, and the best of it is made from grapes grown on a single hill and labeled either Chablis *grand cru* or Chablis *premier cru*, plus usually the name of the vineyard. (See page 21 for names of the seven *grands crus* vineyards.) Wine labeled Chablis or Petit Chablis usually will be of somewhat lesser quality, although very good.

The Beaujolais district produces mostly red wines from the Gamay grape. Nine of the Beaujolais villages are permitted to label their wines *grand cru* with the village name. (See page 29 for the village names.) Wines labeled Beaujolais-Villages are considered in the next category of quality. Below that is Beaujolais Superior, then just plain Beaujolais.

CHAMPAGNE. The province northeast of Paris that is the only region where French champagne may be made. Sparkling wines made elsewhere in France cannot carry this label.

Wine can be made effervescent in several ways, but the only legal way to make champagne is by a complicated and expensive process of fermentation in the bottle—a second fermentation, which manufactures the carbon dioxide gas that produces the pop when the bottle is opened (unless it is opened very carefully) and the bubbles when the wine is poured. Most champagnes are produced from a combination of white and red grapes, primarily the Pinot Noir, Chardonnay, and Pinot Meunier. If the wine is labeled *blanc de noir,* it is made entirely from dark-skinned grapes fermented without the skins. If it is labeled *blanc de blanc,* it is produced entirely from white grapes.

Most champagnes are blends, and most are not made at the vineyard where the grapes are grown. The usual practice is for the grower to sell wine to the shipper, who produces the champagne. The name and reputation of the shipper are important pieces of information in selecting champagne. A few of the well-known shippers are Moet et Chandon, Mumm, Perrier-Jouet, Pommery, and Taittinger.

The best vineyards in the Champagne region are judged by an official rating process and given a grade. Champagne made only from grapes grown in the highest rated vineyards is labeled *grand cru*. The next grade is *premier cru*.

Champagne ranges from very sweet to very dry, and the label will tell you what to expect but not in a straightforward way. In wine language, *sec* ordinarily means dry, but a champagne labeled sec or dry is usually fairly sweet. Champagne labeled extra dry is drier than sec, but it still has more than a trace of sweetness. The driest champagne is labeled *brut* or *nature*. Why this Alice-in-Wonderland labeling? One possible explanation is that many persons believe it is fashionable to drink dry wines but actually prefer sweet ones. They can have it both ways with champagne. Buy a bottle labeled dry and enjoy the sweetness.

ALSACE. A district in northeast France bordering the Rhine, the only French wine region where the name of the grape on the label is more important than a place name. It often indicates a superior wine. The wines are mostly white and usually dry. The two best known are made from the Riesling and Gewurztraminer grapes.

Some Alsatian wines have fairly low alcoholic content. Wines labeled *grand vin, grand reserve, reserve exceptionnelle,* or *grand cru* contain at least 11 percent. *Zwicker* or *Edelzwicker* on the label means a blend of grapes, the latter a blend of superior grapes.

LOIRE VALLEY. A region southwest of Paris along the Loire River that produces good wines of all colors and types. Although no expert would rank the Loire wines with the best of Bordeaux and Burgundy, they can be very pleasant, satisfying wines and are often described as charming and delicious. Except for the sweet varieties, they should be drunk young. Many grape varieties are used including the Chenin Blanc, Sauvignon Blanc, Cabernet Sauvignon, Cabernet Franc, and Muscadet. The major place names on labels include the districts of Anjou and Touraine and the subdistricts of Bourgueil, Chinon, Sancerre, Pouilly, and Vouvray.

Probably the best known of the Loire wines in the United

States is a white wine, Vouvray, made from Chenin Blanc grapes. It can be either sweet or dry. Bourgueil is a red wine made from Cabernet Franc and Cabernet Sauvignon grapes; Chinon is a red wine made from Cabernet Franc grapes. Sancerre and Pouilly-Fume are white wines made from the Sauvignon Blanc grape. (Do not confuse Pouilly-Fume with Pouilly-Fuisse, a white Burgundy made from Chardonnay grapes.) One Loire wine made from the Muscadet or Melon grape is known by the grape name rather than by the name of the place of origin. It is white and dry and highly recommended for serving with fish.

A vast amount of rosé wine comes from the Anjou region, much of it made from the Groslot grape. Some of the best rosés are made from Cabernet Sauvignon.

RHONE VALLEY. A region in southeast France that produces primarly red and rosé wines, along with a very small amount of excellent white wine. The reds are usually described as robust, heady wines with hearty bouquet. They need age in the bottle to reach their potential, and they mature slowly. Some may take ten years or longer. They are usually made from a variety of grapes, possibly twelve or more. One of the principal grapes is the Syrah, which is not the Petite Sirah of California.

The best three areas for red wine are Chateauneuf-du-Pape, Hermitage, and Cote Rotie. The best whites are Condrieu and Chateau Grillet, but only very small amounts are produced. The two best known rosés are Tavel and Lirac.

In addition to the *appellation controlee* wines, there is a second category of French wines labeled V.D.Q.S., *Vins Delimites de Qualite Superieure*. These wines, not widely available in this country, are also produced under official regulations that, although not as strict as the *appellation controlee* regulations, do specify grape varieties and production methods. Below V.D.Q.S. wines are *vin ordinaire* and *vin de pays* (wine of the country), which account for a vast amount of the wine production in France.

German Labels

The quality of French wines may usually be inferred from the geographic origin printed on the label. In general, the smaller and more specific the place of origin, the higher the quality. German labels also report geographic origin, but in addition they carry a quality rating. There are three quality grades: (1) *Tafelwein,* ordinary wine not likely to be on sale in this country; (2) *Qualitatswein,* wine of higher quality that must come from a designated region — an *Anbaugebiete* or *Gebiet* — named on the label; and (3) *Qualitatswein mit Pradikat,* a quality wine with special characteristics. This is the highest category. It, too, must come from a designated region named on the label.

There are six subcategories of *Qualitatswein mit Pradikat,* and the label must show the subcategory. These are *Kabinett, Spatlese* (late harvest), *Auslese* (specially selected bunches), *Beerenauslese* (individually selected grapes), *Trockenbeerenauslese* (grapes left on the vines until nearly dried), and *Eiswein* (wine from frozen grapes). The first five names indicate specific degrees of sweetness. The degree increases in the order named and so, usually, does the price.

All *Qualitatswein mit Pradikat* wines are estate-bottled, and the sweetness must be attained in the natural process of fermentation; none may be added artificially.

All *Qualitatswein* wines must come from one of these eleven regions: Mosel-Saar-Ruwer, Rheingau, Rheinhessen, Rheinpfalz, Ahr, Mittelrhein, Nahe, Hessiche Bergstrasse, Franken, Wurttemberg, and Baden. The great wines of the Mosel-Saar-Ruwer and the Rheingau regions made from the Riesling grapes are considered the best of the German wines.* To name just two wines, the most famous Mosel — if not necessarily the best in every year — is Bernkasteler Doktor and the most famous Rheingau is Schloss Johannisberg.

The major grapes used in German wines are Riesling, the highest in quality but not the best producer, Muller-Thurgau, and Sylvaner.

Wine labeled Liebfraumilch is an exception to the rules explained above. It may be made from a blend from several districts. It is usually sweet, and brands vary from inferior to excellent.

The word *Erzeugerabfullung* on the label means that the wine was bottled by the producer. *Trocken* usually means dry, but in

---

*The name of the German wine region is Mosel-Saar-Ruwer. The river is spelled both Moselle and Mosel, but usually the former spelling is used in France and the latter in Germany. Writers referring in general to the wine rather than the region *usually* write Moselle.

An den steilen
Schieferhängen des
Ockfener Bockstein
Ockfener Herrenberg
Ockfener Geisberg
Saarfeilser Marienberg
liegen die Weinberge des
Weingutes Rheinart-Erben.

Die exponierten Lagen,
besonders aber der
Schiefer, der die Hitze
des Tages aufnimmt und
bei Nacht an die Reben
weitergibt, entwickeln
die feine Art und den
Charakter unserer Weine.

Über 150 Jahre wird im
Weingut Rheinart-Erben
Weinbau an der Saar
betrieben.

Amtl. Prüfungsnummer
3 533 079 15 74

Ⓐ MOSEL-SAAR-RUWER 7256
Ⓑ *Qualitätswein mit Prädikat*
Rheinart Ⓒ
1971er Ⓓ
Ockfener Bockstein Ⓔ
Kabinett Ⓕ
Erzeugerabfüllung Ⓖ
Weingut Adolf Rheinart Erben in Saarburg Ⓗ

GERMAN LABEL

Ⓐ *Region where wine was made*
Ⓑ *Quality wine with special attributes (in this case a Kabinett)*
Ⓒ *Name of producer*
Ⓓ *Year grapes were harvested*
Ⓔ *Name of wine that came from Bockstein vineyard in village of Ockfen*
Ⓕ *One of five quality designations*
Ⓖ *Estate bottled*
Ⓗ *Bottler's name and address*

Trockenbeerenauslese, it means the grapes were dry when picked. The wine itself is very sweet.

In addition to the required information, a German label may list other facts, including the name of a subregion (Bereich); a general site (Grosslage), which is a group of vineyards; or an individual vineyard (Einzellage). This can be confusing, because several of these may have the same word as part of the name. Johannisberg is a village in the Rheingau region, and it is also a subregion, part of the name of the general site, and, in the case of Schloss Johannisberg, an individual vineyard. An excellent source of detailed information about German wines and German labeling is Frank Schoonmaker's *The Wines of Germany,* revised by Peter Sichel.

Italian Labels

Italy is rivaled only by France as a leader in total wine production, and it is by far the largest exporter of wine. As might be expected with heavy production, much Italian wine is ordinary. Some is very good. Few experts would rank Italian wines the equal of the very best French, German, and American wines, but that should not deter any one from drinking them. Obviously it doesn't; more wine is imported into the United States from Italy than from all other European countries combined. Some of the Italian reds in particular are distinguished wines, and some of the whites are very pleasant. In view of their generally lower prices compared with wines of other countries, they are good buys.

Most Italian wines are labeled either with the name of the grape primarily used to make it or the name of its geographic origin. Sometimes both are used. Wines labeled *Denominazione di Origine Controllata* have met standards specified by law and should be of better quality than wines without that designation. Wines labeled *Denominazione di Origine Controllata e Garantita* have been produced under stricter regulations.

Some of the better Italian wines with place names are Barolo, Gattinara, Barbaresco, Valtellina, Ghemme, Bardolino, Valpolicella, Soave, Orvieto, and Frascati. The first seven are red, the others white. Marsala, an amber-colored sweet dessert wine, is named for a city in Sicily.

PRODUCT OF ITALY

RED TABLE WINE

BAROLO Ⓐ

DENOMINAZIONE DI ORIGINE CONTROLLATA Ⓑ

GIRI Ⓒ

1969 Ⓓ

PRODOTTO E IMBOTTIGLIATO NELLA ZONA DI ORIGINE
NELLE CANTINE DELLA
Ⓔ
CONTEA DI CASTIGLIONE
DI
GUIDO GIRI Ⓕ
IN
CASTIGLIONE FALLETTO
CUNEO

ALCOHOL 13.5% BY VOLUME

CONTENTS 1 PT 8 FL. OZS

ITALIAN LABEL

- Ⓐ *Name of wine — the district in which wine was made*
- Ⓑ *Wine meets official standards of quality and origin*
- Ⓒ *Winery*
- Ⓓ *Year grapes were harvested*
- Ⓔ *Produced and bottled by winery in Castiglione township*
- Ⓕ *Producer*

Wines named for the grapes from which they are made include Barbera, Grignolino, Lambrusco, sometimes Nebbiolo, which are red, and Verdicchio, which is white.

Barolo, made from the Nebbiolo grape, is considered the best red wine in Italy by many wine lovers. It is hearty and robust with deep color and distinctive nose, and it requires age to reach its best flavor. Gattinara, made from the same grape, is similar. Barbaresco is also made from the Nebbiolo grape, but it is less robust. Valtellina and Ghemme are also produced from Nebbiolo grapes. Bardolino and Valpolicella are light wines made chiefly from Caroma, Negrara, and Malinara grapes.

Soave may be Italy's best white wine. It is dry, made primarily from Trebbiano and Garganega grapes. Orvieto, made chiefly from Trebbiano grapes, can be sweet or dry.

Lambrusco is the most popular Italian wine in this country. No wine expert would rate it high in quality, but its sweet taste, fruity aroma, and slight sparkle appeal to many people. Barbera is a full-bodied red wine that many persons enjoy with Italian food. Grignolino, a fine wine, is somewhat light in color but usually fairly high in alcohol. Verdicchio is a light white wine often drunk as an accompaniment to fish. It is usually dry, but can be semisweet.

Asti Spumante is probably the most popular imported sparkling wine in the United States. Asti is the name of the Italian town from which the wine originates; *spumante* means sparkling. Made primarily from the Muscat grape, it is usually sweet.

Bianco on an Italian label means white; *rosso*, red; *secco,* dry; and *abboccato* or *amabile,* rather sweet.

The most widely recognized Italian wine name in the United States is probably Chianti, because for many years it was shipped in distinctive straw-covered bottles. There was a time when half of the Italian and many non-Italian restaurants in America were dimly illuminated by candles stuck in empty Chianti bottles.

Chianti is a red wine made from a combination of grapes, chiefly Sangiovese and Canaiolo, which may be very ordinary or very good. *Chianti classico* on the label is an indication of a superior Chianti made in an officially limited region prescribed by law. A few good Chiantis are made in areas outside the *classico* confines, the best of which come from Rufina. Good Chianti, along with Barolo and Gattinara, improves with age. *Riserva* on a Chianti label means the wine is three or more years old.

Chianti is usually shipped now in Bordeaux style bottles without the straw covering. The wine is the same, but some of the appeal is gone.

8. The Fortifieds

THIS book has been concerned primarily with the delights of table wines, which are made to be enjoyed with food. There is another area of delight that should not be overlooked: those wines meant to precede or follow food, the aperitif and dessert wines. If you are planning an evening that you hope will be memorable because of the food, wine, and conversation, consider serving a dry aperitif wine before dinner and a rich, luscious dessert wine at the end. The martini drinkers who want a quick jolt before they eat may not take kindly at first to a fine sherry, but if they can be persuaded to try it, they will find their palates fresher for the good things to follow.

The alcoholic content of table wine is roughly 9 to 14 percent. Aperitif and dessert wines range up to 20 percent or more, because they are fortified with brandy during their vinification. The major fortified wines are sherry, port, Madeira, and Marsala.

Sherry

In Frank Schoonmaker's *Encyclopedia of Wine* (p. 322), sherry is called "beyond question the finest aperitif in the world," and there are many who agree. Schoonmaker adds that it "can be an admirable dessert wine as well."

True sherry comes from a small district surrounding the city of Jerez de la Frontera in Spain, and the name of the wine evolved from the name of the city. If the taste of the wine is unique, and it is, so is the manner in which it is made.

Spanish sherry is blended over a long period of time through a complicated system of oaken casks, called a *solera,* so arranged that wine can be drawn from one cask into the next in the system. New wine enters the first cask, and mature wine is drawn in limited amounts from the last. In this manner wines of various years blend and mature as they move through the solera, and the final product is made up of small amounts of wine from many years.

The principal grape is Palomino, but a number of other grapes are also used.

In general, there are two types of sherry, fino and oloroso. The former is developed with a special yeast, called *flor,* which imparts a distinctive flavor. Finos tend to be pale, delicate, and dry and are usually drunk as aperitifs. Olorosos are full-bodied, darker in color, usually higher in alcohol, and often sweetened with the juice of the Pedro Ximenez grapes.

There are many sherries. In color they range from pale to amber to gold to the very dark, called brown sherry. All sherries are dry in the beginning, but some are sweetened, particularly those intended for the export trade.

Sherries are often labeled with brand names, which unfortunately do not always indicate the type of sherry in the bottle, but you may find fino or oloroso or some other descriptive name on the label. A Manzanilla, made in an area adjoining the sherry district, is a very pale fino, light, dry, somewhat tart. Amontillado is slightly darker, usually dry although sometimes sweetened, with a prominent nutty flavor. A cream sherry is a sweetened oloroso.

The story of sherry is long and colorful. During the era of sailing ships, casks of sherry were loaded on ships and sent to the East Indies and back. It was thought the motion of the ship improved and matured the wine, and the much-traveled product was known as East Indies Sherry.

Wine labeled sherry is produced in a number of other countries, including the United States, but American regulations are so permissive, there is no guarantee that an American sherry will remotely resemble one from Spain. A few American sherries are good, authentic in taste; others are not really sherry at all. Try Concannon Prelude or Christian Brothers Dry Sherry.

Port

If sherry is the finest aperitif wine, then port must be the most famous dessert wine. You can buy wine labeled port made in many countries, but true port comes from Portugal. It is made from grapes heavy with sugar, including the Touriga, the Bastardo, and the Tintas. During the vinification, grape brandy is mixed with the must. This stops the fermentation while there is still a high sugar content and results in a sweet wine with an alcoholic content of 19 percent or more.

Port is usually made by blending wines from several years. Only in an exceptionally good year is a port made entirely from grapes harvested in a single year. This becomes a vintage port, one of the two instances (champagne is the other) when the word *vintage* on a label means an outstanding wine. Vintage port requires a long time in the bottle to reach its peak, at least ten or fifteen years and often longer.

Vintage port usually develops a heavy sediment or crust inside the bottle. To remove it, the wine should be decanted very carefully before drinking or filtered through a napkin or paper coffee filter.

Most of the nonvintage ports are aged longer before bottling and are ready to drink by the time they are available in the United States. There are two general types: ruby, the younger of the two, deep red in color with a flavor often described as fruity; and tawny, which has more age and, as the name indicates, a darker, brownish color. Tawny is usually considered the better, but both can be very good. There is also a white port, but it is not of the same quality. Among the historic bottlers and shippers of port are Dows, Sandeman, Graham, and Cockburn.

A vast amount of wine labeled port is produced in the United States, but, as with sherry, the regulations are so permissive, it may or may not bear any resemblance to true port. In some instances it is made in the same manner as Portuguese port and is very good. One we have tried and recommend is the moderately priced Paul Masson's Rare Souzao. It is made from a Portuguese grape, Souzao, with blue black, intensely pigmented skins that give the wine a wonderfully deep color.

Unhappily some American-labeled port resembles real port in only one respect—its alcoholic content. It is ironic that the same name is applied to both a sublime after dinner drink and the daily diet of skid row winos.

American laws do require that port made in this country be so labeled. And Portugal requires that port exported to the United States be labeled Porto.

Madeira

This wine takes its name from the Portuguese island in the Atlantic where it originated. It is a fortified dessert or aperitif wine with a taste quite different from port or sherry, due in part to its being kept for months at a very high temperature. As with sherry, in its early days, it was thought a sea voyage improved it, and Madeira was shipped to India and back before being marketed. The American colonists enjoyed Madeira, convinced it was improved by the voyage to the Atlantic seaboard.

Madeiras vary widely from very dry to very sweet. Most of the better ones are labeled with the name of the grapes from which they are made, and the name is an indication of sweetness. Madeira labeled Sercial, from the Sercial grape, is the dryest. Boal is much sweeter, and the sweetest of all is Malmsey from the grape of that name.

One type of Madeira, rainwater, is not named for a grape. It takes its name from the fact that it is very light and pale in color. It is usually dry.

Marsala

Marsala is the Italian dessert wine made in the city of Marsala in Sicily. Amber in color, it may be either dry or sweet. It is made as a dry wine from white grapes, fortified with brandy and, to make a sweet wine, sweetened with concentrated grape juice.

Each aperitif and dessert wine has a distinctive taste, different from all of the others. Each is different from any table wine. We have avoided trying to describe these tastes. One sip is worth a dozen adjectives.

9. Screw Caps and Short Corks

J U G   W I N E S are the *vin ordinaire* of America. Europeans, the French particularly, have always known of the symbiotic affinity of food and wine. They do not regard this relationship with awe. The bottle of table wine has the same status as the mustard pot or the pepper mill. It's just a part of the meal. It's watered a bit for the children, which leaves an extra glass for *pere.*

In France these wines are delivered to homes, grocery stores, and small cafes in one-liter bottles, much as milk is delivered in this country. The bottles are filled from barrels or tanks and are capped with the same ceramic and spring-wire seal that Grandpa used on his homemade root beer. None of this is done under operating room conditions, but it is not expected that the wine will have a prolonged life in the bottle. The spring-loaded cap allows the bottle to be restoppered, and it is assumed the contents will be consumed within a few days.

There are no exact American counterparts to the French *vin ordinaire,* no friendly neighborhood wine routes, no freshly capped bottles of wine readily available. But we do have jug wines. By our definition they may or may not actually come in jugs. We define them as inexpensive wines that have screw caps or short corks, come primarily from California, and usually have generic labels. At this writing they are priced at $4 or less in the 750 ml size and about $6 for the 1½ l size. (We hope you will recognize the necessity of adjusting these prices if inflation continues.)

Jug wines are not bottled locally for immediate consumption; so certain procedures are necessary if they are to remain stable on store shelves and survive opening and reopening over a period of several days.

Air spoils wine, and quickly too. Oxidation not only accelerates degrading chemical processes, but bacteria and other microorganisms also begin to flourish. There are several measures of protection against these hazards. Most important, the screw cap, which seals the wine adequately until the bottle is opened, can be replaced easily to reduce the exposure to air during storage. The short cork although less convenient than the screw cap, is easier to replace than the long cork of premium wines.

The wine may be protected from microorganisms by pasteurization. This is essentially the same rapid heat treatment our milk supply undergoes. And just as pasteurization somewhat alters the taste of milk, so does it tend to dull some of the attributes of wine. Wine may be protected from wild organisms by treating it with sulphur. This is most effective against yeasts, and, if artfully done, is not usually detected. Occasionally the wine may have been overtreated and have a burned-kitchen-match aroma and taste. This should disappear with a little exposure in the glass. If it doesn't, then too much sulphur is really too much.

The wine may be protected to a moderate extent by chemical antioxidants and preservatives, such as sorbates. These additives may prevent oxidation for a while, but in excess they will give the wine a sort of bubble-gum nose and flavor. This may be fine if you are eight to twelve years old; for an adult this cloying, sweet, cosmeticlike quality is disagreeable.

The final protection is cold. Any partly emptied bottle of jug wine or any other table wine should be tightly reclosed and refrigerated pending subsequent use.

As the planting of great wine grapes has expanded in California over the last two decades, the quality of jug wines has continued to improve. They are now the vinous bargains of the world, a vast improvement over the French mealtime glass of wine. To be sure, the "Burgundy" tastes nothing like Burgundy, and the "Chablis" has nothing in common with Chablis. "Chianti" hasn't an Italian grape in the entire tank, and "Rhine" wines may have an indifferent association with the Riesling grape. Nonetheless, some of these are very good.

Among the reds we have enjoyed are Gallo's Hearty Burgundy and Chianti, Taylor California Cellars Burgundy, Fetzer's Mendocino Red, Louis Martini's Zinfandel, Robert Mondavi's Red Table Wine, and Sebastiani's Burgundy.

The whites are enjoying great popularity now. When an indifferent customer orders "a glass of Chablis, please" from the bar, we have often wondered what the reaction would be if the bartender served a glass of *grand cru* Blanchots — at a charge of $40 for the bottle. In jug wine language, Chablis has come to mean any reasonably dry white wine. Some of those we have enjoyed are Taylor California Cellars Chablis, Paul Masson Chablis, Robert Mondavi White, Sebastiani Mountain Chablis, Beaulieu California Chablis, Gallo Chablis Blanc, and Christian Brothers California Chablis.

Rosé wines have a growing popularity (a lot more pink champagne is sold than you might suspect). We will mention only two, which in their own way are unique. Gallo Pink Chablis (the very name is a contradiction) is a quite nice, fresh, handsome luncheon wine. The attractive color and brisk taste lend a pleasant touch to a bridal luncheon shower. The other is Christian Brothers La Salle Rosé. This wine represents a curve ball that Brother Timothy served up to the Bureau of Alcohol, Tobacco, and Firearms. This fairly new bureaucracy (which may by now be reorganized) is the IRS of the wine world. Champagne bears an extra tax because it is effervescent. So Brother Timothy, the cellar master, made up an eye-catching, fresh rosé and allowed it to contain enough bubbles to prickle your tongue, but not enough to qualify for extra taxation as a sparkling wine. This *petillant* wine is a luncheon picnic delight.

Although most jug wines carry generic labels, increasingly they are being compounded of respectable wine grapes instead of the heavy-producing but low-quality grapes from which they once were made. The burgeoning supply of fine varietal grapes has greatly elevated quality. For example, here is how Dr. Richard Peterson of Monterey Vineyards compounded three generic wines in 1977 and 1978:

> **Classic Red:** Cabernet Sauvignon 60 percent, Pinot Noir 10 percent, Zinfandel 30 percent. (These three fine varieties speak for themselves.)
> **Classic Rosé:** Napa Gamay 18 percent, Pinot Noir 8 percent, Grenache 47 percent, Cabernet Sauvignon 17.5 percent,

Grey Riesling 9 percent, Zinfandel 0.5 percent. (These are all fine wine grapes except for Grey Riesling, and Dr. Peterson said,"We thought it added something to our blend, so there it is.")

Classic Dry White: Pinot Blanc 37 percent, French Columbard 27 percent, Chenin Blanc 28 percent, Grey Riesling 8 percent.

Jug wines are a mixture of wines to a taste, not to a recipe, so these may be one-time percentages that are not intended to hold from year to year. Part of the art lies in maintaining a standard product made from highly variable materials.

Recently a few winemakers, aided by Madison Avenue skill in telling us that a lesser product is better for us, have introduced a new product called light wines. Low in alcohol and supposedly low in calories, they represent a trendy approach to the market pioneered by light Scotch, light American whiskey, light beer, and diet drinks.

Until regulations were changed recently, it was illegal to call an American-made beverage wine if it contained less than 9 percent alcohol. This constraint was lifted so domestic wines could compete with certain low-alcohol German wines, which are, incidentally, quite pallid, in our estimation.

Currently there are two techniques for producing domestic light wine. The first is to pick the grapes before they are mature when they contain less sugar. This results, after fermentation, in a lower alcohol and caloric content. With most grape varieties, full flavor is obtained only from ripe grapes, but there are exceptions. Chardonnay may produce fresh, fruity wines (such as champagne) from early-picked berries and quite different, mouth-filling table wines from fully ripened grapes. Light wines made from certain grapes by this technique can be crisp and fresh when chilled, but they are still a pale shadow of their orthodox counterparts.

With the second technique, fully ripened, high-sugar grapes are fermented into wines of normal alcohol levels, and some of the alcohol is then removed by boiling it off in a vacuum. This process is a relative of the freeze-dry process used to produce instant coffee.

Sometimes a third type of light wine is produced by the artful blending of wines made by these two processes. In a recent blind tasting, there was unanimous agreement that the wines blended from the two processes were superior to the others. Those preferred were from Taylor California Cellars, Paul Masson, and Los Hermanos.

Any light wine is drinkable, but don't expect pronounced flavor and don't expect to lose weight. Most table wines are already low in calories, usually about 75 per glass. Light wines average about 25 percent less. That may sound impressive until you run the figures through your pocket calculator. If you enjoy two glasses of wine with your evening meal, and if you substitute light wine, you will decrease your caloric intake by about 37½ calories per day or 13,687 in a year. That translates into a weight loss of about .009 of a pound in a day or 3.3 pounds in a year.

Most light wines are a bit more expensive than their counterparts, and, at this writing, no very reliable light red wines have been marketed.

To summarize on jug wines, we recommend them — except for light wines — for daily consumption. You will be better served than your French friends, and you will save enough to buy that magnificent single bottle for a special occasion.

When dealing with your own "house wines" there are three things to remember: (1) most of them are better, even the reds, when at least somewhat chilled because cold conceals many imperfections; (2) the unused portion should be kept under refrigeration; and (3) unused wine should be transferred if possible to a smaller sealed container. It is the quantity of air in the bottle that destroys the wine.

You will enjoy sipping your way through the jug wine section of your favorite supplier until you find your own favorite "house wines."

A votre sante!

10. The Corkscrew, the Glass, and What Goes with What

 A F T E R telling you how to select a wine, some wine books give precise, detailed instructions on how to store it, open it, pour it, and serve it. We are inclined to be permissive on these housekeeping details, but a few suggestions and a rule or two may be helpful.

Storing

Ideally, wine should be stored in a cool, dark place free of vibration. Heat speeds the aging process and hampers a wine's proper development. Premium wines stored in a warm place will not last long and may never reach their potential. A temperature of 50 to 60°F. is best, and consistency of temperature is as important as the temperature level. Sudden, sharp changes have adverse effects.

If you have such a storage area, you can buy good wines when they are young and easily available, and keep them until they are ready for drinking. By that time they may be difficult to find in wine shops and much higher in price. If you don't have a cool, dark place, choose the coolest spot you can find and don't try to hold your wines for a long period.

Bottles of premium wine must be stored on their sides so the corks will remain moist. This is the one hard rule in wine housekeeping. If a cork dries and shrinks, air will enter the bottle and spoil the wine.

Jug wines don't improve with age so there is no reason to lay them away for a long period. And if a bottle has a screw cap, there is no reason to place it on its side; the cap won't deteriorate standing up.

Opening

Anyone old enough to buy wine has been exposed to a corkscrew and probably doesn't need advice on how to extract a cork from a bottle, but here are a few tips.

Most bottles have a foil or plastic cap covering the cork. Cut this below the level of the bottle's top or remove it entirely, so the wine will not touch the foil or plastic as it is poured and pick up specks of dirt or musty odors held under the cap. Wipe the top of the bottle's neck to remove any mold or dirt. Then draw the cork.

There is a trick to opening a champagne bottle. Wrap it in a towel to protect your hands in case the bottle should explode. An explosion isn't likely, but it has happened. Hold the bottle at a forty-five-degree angle so there will be more room for the gas to escape when the cork is out and less likelihood that the wine will shoot up like a fountain. Point the bottle away from yourself and any guests. Remove the foil, exposing the wire cage over the cork. Remove the wire by twisting the tab until it breaks. Hold the bottle firmly with one hand and the cork firmly with the other. Twist the bottle slowly while gently working out the cork. If you do this carefully, the cork will come out silently in your hand. Allowing it to shoot across the room with a loud pop will be more spectacular, but it will also spill a lot of champagne and cause the bubbles to escape.

If you are buying a new corkscrew, get one that looks like a spiral wire coil sharply pointed at the lower end. Do not buy one that is a solid, tapered piece of metal with flanges on the edge, somewhat resembling a wood screw. If you are dealing with a tightly corked bottle, the latter will bore a hole in the cork, but it won't grasp it firmly enough to pull it out. The bit should be at least two inches long, so it will penetrate long corks.

Corkscrews are available with a wide range of levering arrangements to draw corks easily and smoothly. If you don't like corkscrews, there are other devices to remove corks. One has a long tube that is punched through the cork to squirt air into the bottle, thereby forcing the cork out. Another consists of two thin metal tines that are inserted between the cork and the bottle and twisted to release the cork. They all work; it's a matter of personal preference.

Pouring and Serving

Many conventions have grown up around the pouring and serving of wine; some of them pleasant and useful, some pointless or pretentious. There is no need to make an elaborate ceremony of serving wine except, perhaps, when you are sharing a rare, old, expensive bottle with appreciative friends.

Open the bottle, taste it to be sure it hasn't deteriorated, bring it to the table, pour a few ounces in each glass, and place the bottle upright on the table where it will be handy when you want to pour again. If there are more than five or six guests you may want to place a second bottle at the end of the table opposite the host or hostess, perhaps asking a guest to help in the pouring.

Some hosts and hostesses like to pour wine into a decanter before serving, either because they think the decanter looks better than a bottle or because they are uncomfortable about the wine they are serving and prefer not to disclose its identity. We think a wine bottle, which usually has a colorful label, adds an attractive touch to the table, particularly when standing in a silver wine coaster.

There are, however, occasions when a decanter should be used. One is when a jug wine is being served, and the bottle is too large to leave on the table. Another is when you are serving a very old wine that has thrown a sediment in the bottle. In that case careful decanting is a necessity. Stand the bottle upright a day before serving if possible, to allow the sediment to settle. Draw the cork just before serving and pour the wine slowly into a decanter, holding the bottle in front of a strong light so you can see when all of the clear liquid has been poured. Stop pouring, of course, before any of the sediment can drain into the decanter. An alternative to standing the bottle upright for a time is to draw the cork while holding the bottle as nearly as possible in the same position in which it was stored.

Wrapping a towel around the bottle while pouring is a useless gesture, bordering on the pretentious, unless the bottle is wet from chilling. Carry a napkin, if you wish, to take care of spills, but don't hide the bottle. Many guests will be interested in knowing what wine they are drinking, and it is a gracious touch to keep the bottle visible. A slight twist of the bottle as you finish each pouring will usually prevent dripping.

Red wines should be served at room temperature, which means something less than 75 degrees if you live in an overheated apartment. White wines should be chilled either in a refrigerator or in a wine cooler placed on the table or beside the host's chair.

Don't waste money on a wicker basket. It is of no use in carrying a bottle from the storage area, and resting a bottle in a basket at the table serves no purpose except to waste space.

Now about the practice of opening a bottle an hour or two before serving so the wine can "breathe." If you read a few wine books, you will soon learn that wine writers, like economists, freqently disagree. Breathing is a subject on which they disagree strongly. Some contend that allowing a bottle of red wine to stand with the cork drawn for an hour or two before serving greatly improves the wine. We don't think so.

It is true that wines change after exposure to air. In the case of a mature wine, the aromas developed from the fruit acids and other elements are released, producing a delightful bouquet. But it seems to us unrealistic to think that the square inch of space in the neck of an opened bottle will aerate its contents in a short interval and produce a pronounced change. The place for a wine to breathe is in the wine glass, where broad exposure to air exists. This, along with the aeration from pouring, is all the exposure a good wine needs.

If a wine needs more exposure than this—a young, harsh, immature wine may benefit by a rounding off of its sharp edges— decant it first and then pour it. The act of decanting will give it plenty of air exposure quickly and may dissipate some of the harshness. A word of caution about decanting an old wine: Too much exposure to air may cause it to lose its complexity, its delicate nuances. It may destroy its elegance.

The Iowa Wine Advisory Board conducted one experiment on breathing that, although not extensive enough to be considered scientific, provided an interesting result. Two bottles each of ten different, relatively good Bordeaux wines were tasted. From one set of ten, the corks were drawn two hours before tasting. Corks were drawn from the other set just before tasting. All bottles were placed

Left, all-purpose glass for table wine. Right, champagne flute.

in paper sacks so none of the tasters knew which had breathed, which had not. The result: Nine of the ten wines were preferred with freshly drawn corks. One wine, a fairly young Medoc, was preferred after breathing.

To recap: Old wines lose by aeration, young wines may be helped a bit, prime wines may suffer. And we don't believe wines breathe in an hour or two through an open bottle neck.

As we pointed out in the first chapter of this book, a special glass has been designed for each type of table wine — red Burgundy, white Burgundy, claret, Moselle, Rhine wines, champagne — for dessert wines, and so on. If you want to be a traditionalist, you can find the various types illustrated in brochures and charts available in many stores that sell glassware.

You can do very well with one all-purpose glass. It should be stemmed, so you can hold it by the stem and enjoy the color of the wine. It should be tulip-shaped, with a smaller diameter at the top than at the bottom, so the aroma will be concentrated in the glass. It should hold as much as eight ounces or more if filled to the top, so that three or four ounces can be poured at a serving, leaving plenty of space to be filled by the aroma. It should be made of clear glass, so nothing obstructs or distorts the play of light on the wine.

Don't serve wine in colored glasses unless they are a priceless family treasure that you want to display to your friends.

You may want to use somewhat smaller glasses for aperitif and dessert wines if you serve them often, although they will taste fine in the all-purpose glass.

A tip about serving champagne. Don't use those saucer-shaped glasses often pictured in adds for New Year's Eve festivities. The wide surface encourages the bubbles to evaporate, leaving the wine flat. If you want special glasses for champagne buy the tall, thin tulip-shaped glasses, called *flutes*.

In a Restaurant

Do your palms grow cold and sweaty when you are handed a wine list and asked, "Would you care to select a wine to accompany your dinner?"

Relax! The chances are fairly even the waiter knows less about wine than you do. His job usually is to sell you a bottle.

There are a couple of safe ploys. "What would you suggest?" is a standard opening and may very quickly uncover the extent of the knowledge gap. If an officious, slightly insulting attitude develops, it is best to inquire, "Does the house have a special list of a few other bottles not included here?" This question has a way of clearing the air.

A good bit of foolishness can go on in a restaurant in the serving of wine, but not all of the ritual is pointless. If you are in an inexpensive or moderately priced restaurant and order a carafe of wine, the carafe will be brought and placed on your table, and that's that. No ceremony. Before you order you may want to ask what wine is being used as the carafe wine, but don't expect to be shown the bottle.

If you order a specific wine from the wine list, the bottle should be brought to you before it is opened, so you can see that you are getting what you ordered. Check the vintage date, too, to be sure it is the same one listed on the wine card. If the bottle already has been opened, don't accept it.

A small amount of wine should be poured in your glass to be sampled before the guests are served. If you have ordered something more than a *vin ordinaire,* this is not an affectation; you want to be sure the wine is in good condition. If you have ordered something in the jug wine category making a ritual of tasting is silly. Signal the waiter to get on with the pouring.

Your wine order may be taken by the regular waiter or by a wine steward. In expensive restaurants the wine steward may be called the sommelier and will probably be decorated with a chain around the neck bearing a key, presumably to the cellar, or a tasting cup. If it is a good restaurant rather than just a pretentious one, the sommelier will be knowledgeable and can usually be trusted to make sensible suggestions, if you want them, about wines in your price bracket to accompany the food you are ordering. Be advised, however, that we have seen persons dressed as sommeliers in pseudoelegant motel restaurants along interstate highways, and their knowledge of wine was on a par with the busboy's.

Sometimes a wine card is more entertaining than informative. In a Holiday Inn restaurant, we found this description of a French white wine: "Inoffensive, pale, light, crisp, dry, and with no trace of acidity." We didn't order it. "Bring us something offensive," we said.

One caveat about returning a bottle of wine in a restaurant: If you are sure it is spoiled, or too old, or not what it is represented as being, send it back. A reputable restaurant will accept your judgment without argument. But be sure you are right. Very, very few bottles in a good restaurant's cellar are spoiled. If you are in doubt ask the wine steward or the manager to sample the wine with you.

Wine with Food

With so many different wines to choose from — red, white, rosé, sweet, dry, sparkling, still — how does a person select one wine to accompany food? There are a few general guidelines. They are not hard rules to be followed slavishly, but there is a reason for them. They represent the cumulative judgment of wine drinkers over a long period of time.

In general, serve red wine with red meat, and the more robust the meat, the heartier the wine. With a thick juicy steak, try a robust Bordeaux or Cabernet Sauvignon or a Barolo. With an aromatic stew, try a Zinfandel or a Rhone wine. Pasta dishes with meat or meat sauces usually go well with Barbera or Chianti.

In general, serve white wine with white meat, fish, and fowl.

With shellfish, the drier whites are usually best. The classic wines with oysters and clams are Chablis, Chardonnay, and Muscadet, but if you use a California Chablis, be sure it is dry. Wines not quite as dry—Riesling, for example—go well with some other fish dishes. Our favorite wine with pork is a spicy Gewurztraminer. If you are serving a pasta dish without meat, try a Soave or an Orvieto. Some fowl will take light red wines as well as white. We usually serve Beaujolais with our Thanksgiving turkey. Game—roast duck for example—will often be better with red wines than with white. Nothing goes better with lobster than champagne. Nothing goes better with champagne than lobster.

In general, serve dry wines with food and sweet wines after dinner. But a sweet Sauternes is delightful with many desserts.

If you want to serve both red and white wine, serve the white first with a soup or other first course. The white after the red will seem weak. (This does not apply to a white dessert wine at the end of the meal.) If you want to serve two reds, serve the younger or lighter before the older or heavier. If you serve the former last it will seem thin.

In general, when serving the fortified wines serve the dry ones before dinner—the dry sherries and dry Madeiras—and the sweet ones—port, sweet Madeira, sweet sherry—after dinner or with dessert. Occasionally an aperitif wine will go well with a soup course. Sherry with turtle soup is a classic combination. So is Madeira.

In general, don't serve any wine with salads containing vinegar or with citrus fruits or anchovies. Some books tell you not to serve wine with chocolate, but we recently were served a fine Sauternes with chocolate mousse, and we thought they went together very well.

So much for the general guidelines. Follow them, and you will be on safe ground. As you become familiar with the characteristics of different wines, a better approach is to think about which wines seem most appropriate in taste, body, aroma, etc., with the food in question. A beginning cook follows a recipe precisely. An experienced cook improvises to arrive at a harmonious but not bland, enticing combination of flavors. So it is with wine and food.

11.   Two Stories, Each with a Moral

A S   with most pleasures there is no exact measure for the enjoyment of wine. And despite all of the information we have given you in this book, there is no precise yardstick for judging a wine's quality. The mysteries of the grapes and the vagaries of human reaction are always present. Here are two personal experiences of one of the authors, Tom Throckmorton.

SEVERAL YEARS AGO I was motoring with friends in the Basque country of southwestern France. This is the land of peaked berets, D'Artagnan, and cigarettes pasted to lower lips. At noon we found ourselves in the village of Plaisance and noted the Hotel La Ripa Alta had a single Michelin star. A picturesque country inn, it had a quiet dining room with dark wood, gleaming crystal, and a cherubic chef who had formerly been the chef on the steamship *Normandie*.

Our meal began with whole truffled and glazed livers of duck and goose. Elegant, firm slices were accompanied by a very satisfactory sweet Jurancon. The main course was a distinguished saddle of lamb, presented with flair, carved with artistry, and served unobtrusively. The accompanying wine was a Madiran. None of us was familiar with it. The bouquet was lovely and full, resembling a Cabernet Sauvignon blended with a little Beaujolais. The color was deep purple and young, but on the tongue were great tastes of fresh fruit, an appealing vinosity, and only enough tannin to notice. It was a beautiful wine and went magnificently with the juicy slices of pink lamb. We ignored the salad and went to the local cheeses, which brought out every great quality of the Madiran.

As we lingered over the wine and cheese, the chef joined us for a glass and some engaging conversation. The luncheon ended with three varieties of homemade fruit sorbets and a single glass of extra dry champagne to clear our throats and heads.

The Madiran was the principal topic of conversation during and after the meal. We had discovered a little known and truly outstanding French country wine. We all vowed to order a couple of cases.

And indeed we did.

And on another memorable evening, we met to sample our newly arrived Madiran. You may be foreseeing the end of this. The wine was strictly ho-hum. The ambience of a French country luncheon with good friends had warped our judgment. We had equated the pleasures of Plaisance with the quality of the wine. I do not feel unhappy, however. It has happened to others, and it may someday happen to you.

The Wine Advisory Board has often been besieged by friends to help obtain "that marvelous wine we had along the coast of Yugoslavia. We brought the label home, but no one seems to know it."

The explanation is easy — a relaxed vacation, a breathtaking view down the Dalmatian coast, unusual foods well prepared and graciously served, unhurried conversation with engaging friends or charming strangers. The delightful luncheon and the gold and blue afternoon were memorable; and so, of course, was the otherwise very ordinary wine.

THE MORAL OF THIS STORY:
Substance isn't everything. Food fills the stomach, but style and ambience add joy to the heart.

LOUIS MARTINI once invited the great and near great of the wine world to a tasting of all of his Cabernet Sauvignon vintages back to the late 1940s. The bottles were wrapped to conceal their labels. After the wines were tasted and scored, many of the tasters were able to place them in fairly accurate chronologic order. But no one discerned the ringer that Mr. Martini had inserted in the line-up, a beautifully matured bottle of Zinfandel.

I witnessed a somewhat similar happening. I had just discovered the true greatness of California wines. Mario Gemello, working in a little winery behind the bowling alley in Mountain View, California, had produced the most satisfying California Cabernet Sauvignon I had tasted, a 1960 vintage. I Christmas-wrapped a bottle for a friend in St. Louis. We were both attending a meeting of the St. Louis chapter of the Commanderie de Bordeaux, a wine society dedicated to the enjoyment, appreciation, and worship of only Bordeaux wines.

As a joke, I suggested to my friend that sometime he might wish to serve the Gemello to a wine snob acquaintance. He suggested, instead, that we serve it that evening — to the head table. There sat one of the world's wine authorities, an importer, scholar, and author. At his elbow was the owner of one of the foremost chateaux of St. Emilion. There also were the Grand Maitre of the Order and the official family of the St. Louis chapter.

The bottle was delivered and tasted while still wrapped. At once it was the subject of an intense argument. The international wine expert pronounced it a 1959 Haut Brion. The St. Emilion winemaker was equally certain it was a 1962 Mouton Rothschild. Each explained his reasons. The rest of the table chose up sides.

When the wrapping was removed it was as if a handsome young bastard had walked uninvited into a family reunion. There were gasps of amazement and horrified side glances. Suddenly the offending bottle was ignored, and I noted a frosty coolness toward my friend and me. Previously I had invited the world-renowned expert to breakfast on the following morning. He had accepted, but I was subsequently informed that he had changed his plans and taken an earlier plane.

THE MORAL OF THIS STORY:
When you become an expert, hold on to a touch of humility. You may be wrong.

12. A Look into the Future

 A M E R I C A N S are far behind Europeans in the pleasant custom of enjoying wine regularly with meals, but there are portents of change. And from a strange quarter. It is likely that widespread appreciation of wine in this country will be brought to us by the Kool-Aid generation. Shortly after World War II, our booming younger generation became addicted to Kool-Aid, a highly colored, sweetened, artificially flavored fruit drink. Prepared by mixing the contents of a small envelope with water and a few ice cubes, the beverage flowed down children's throats in veritable floods. Parents approved of the stuff because it was inexpensive, contained no caffeine, and tended to keep the kids away from the drugstore and out of mischief.

Then came the liberal, laid-back 60s, and the generation began looking for an identity, an escape from the middle class morality of the Establishment. Someone made a bland wine from Thompson Seedless grapes, added artificial colorings and fruit flavors, and overnight liberated an entire generation from the bondage of their elders. Boone's Farm, Annie Green Springs, and a hundred other "fruit wines" made the scene, most of them relatively low in alcoholic content.

There was a certain synergism between these sweet wines and marijuana. Viet Nam was there to hate. Endless philosophical discussions were fueled by these strange drinks, wines that bore no relation to food or meals, but rather served as lubricants for social gatherings. They helped compose the loudly vehement music of a generation, and they helped millions identify with amplified strings, constant percussion, and resentful lyrics.

Another decade passed and the issue of Viet Nam went away, communes drifted apart, old values were reviewed, and new responsibilities were assumed. The fruit wines were part of a past life, and the Kool-Aid generation discovered Lambrusco. This dark purple, fresh, sweetish, slightly sparkling wine is filled with tastes. And it *can* be drunk with food—at least with some foods and by some individuals. So a whole generation has now been weaned away from artificial wines to a type of real wine and is beginning to drink it with luncheon and dinner.

The importance of this shift can be converted into numbers: Nearly as much Lambrusco wine was imported into the United States in 1980 as all of the imports of French and German wines combined. The total was more than 21 million gallons! Therein lies our greatest hope of becoming a nation truly appreciative of wine.

Certainly some day someone in the Kool-Aid generation, if only by accident, will pick up a bottle of good honest table wine. Perhaps it will be a great mouth-filling, mind-blowing, lusty Zinfandel. By chance it will be drunk with a meal, and suddenly a humdrum pot roast will become a royal banquet. The truth—that table wines are as much a part of dining as the entree or the tea or the coffee—will dawn. The color, the bouquet, and the complex taste will be fascinating topics of conversation at a table habitually silent.

The word will leak out to the other millions of the Kool-Aid generation. The use of wine to heighten the enjoyment of food and company will not remain a secret. Wine shops will be besieged, and restaurant wine lists will lengthen as patrons discover the infinite variety of wine.

It costs less to make a liter of wine than to produce a liter of milk, but through the strange convolutions of morality, wine has been considered sinful. Therefore, it must be taxed, and the tax has made it seem a luxury. Wine is a food, like milk; it belongs on the dining table as part of the meal.

The Kool-Aid generation is experienced in social upheaval. It could very well create one in wine.

13.   Let's Talk about It

TALLEYRAND, the French diplomat, was instructing a young man in the proper way to approach a famous Burgundy. No one can be sure of the exact words, but the conversation went something like this:

"First, we hold the glass to the light and admire the color," said Talleyrand.

"Yes," said the young man.

"Then we hold the glass to the nose and inhale the aroma."

"Yes," said the young man eagerly, "and then?"

"Then we put down the glass and talk about it."

For centuries people have been talking about wine—poets, philosophers, peasants, priests—and some of what they have said has been memorable.

Probably the most famous quotation in wine history is the rapturous statement attributed to Dom Pierre Perignon, a seventeenth-century monk who was the cellar master of a Benedictine Abbey in France. The legend is that he "invented" champagne, which probably isn't quite true, but the fact is that he was among the first to experiment with corks for closing bottles. Fermentation in the bottles created gas, and the corks held the gas in the bottles, making the wine effervescent. Tradition has it that one day after opening his first corked bottle Dom Perignon, who was blind, called to his colleagues, "Oh, come quickly! I am drinking stars!"[1]

---

1. Harold J. Grossman, *Grossman's Guide to Wines, Spirits, and Beers* (New York: Charles Scribner's Sons, 1964), 16.

A somewhat different reaction to champagne is attributed to Art Buchwald, the columnist, who said, "I like champagne, because it always tastes as though my foot's asleep."[2]

Many famous persons, along with the wine industry, have contended fervently that wine is actually food. No one said it with more brevity or conviction than did Oliver Wendell Holmes when he said, "Wine is a food!"[3]

Louis Pasteur, the first to understand the fermentation process, thought wine was more healthful for adults than milk. He declared, "Wine can be considered with good reason to be the most healthful and the most hygienic of all beverages."[4] Considering the quality of milk in his day, he was undoubtedly right.

And in 1 Tim. 5:23, Paul had this advice: "Drink no longer water, but use a little wine for thy stomach's sake and thine often infirmities."

Not everyone would agree that wine is healthful. Perhaps the most unhealthy experience with wine known to us occurred in the fifteenth century when George, Duke of Clarence, younger brother of King Edward IV, drowned in a butt of Malmsey.[5]

Some writers have praised wine effusively for its magic enhancement of life's pleasures. Samuel Johnson said, "Wine gives great pleasure and every pleasure is of itself a good."[6] A somewhat similar thought was expressed by Goethe: "Wine rejoices the heart of man, and joy is the mother of all virtue."[7]

James Joyce wrote, with a touch of realism tempering his romanticism: "What is better than to sit at the end of the day and drink wine with friends, or substitutes for friends."[8]

Dumas, speaking of the superb Burgundy Chambertin, said: "Nothing inspires such a rosy view of the future."[9]

---

2. Alexis Lichine, *New Encyclopedia of Wine and Spirits,* 161.
3. Frank Schoonmaker, *Encyclopedia of Wine,* 179.
4. Lichine, *New Encyclopedia,* 25.
5. Schoonmaker, *Encyclopedia of Wine,* 217.
6. Ibid., 193.
7. Ruth Ellen Church, *The American Guide to Wines* (Illinois: Quadrangle, 1963), 91.
8. Alexis Bespaloff, *The Fireside Book of Wine* (New York: Simon and Schuster, 1977), 19.
9. Lichine, *New Encyclopedia,* 129.

9 2

John Wesley, the founder of Methodism, made a comment that must puzzle some of his Prohibitionist descendants: "Wine is one of the noblest cordials in nature."[10]

And Benjamin Franklin, who learned to enjoy wine in France, found religious comfort in the glass: "Wine . . . a constant proof that God loves us and loves to see us happy."[11]

Duff Cooper, British statesman and author, wrote: "Wine has lit up for me the pages of literature, and revealed in life romance lurking in the commonplace."[12]

And from the Bible again (Ps. 104:15): "Wine that maketh glad the heart of man."

Thomas Jefferson, wine lover and grape grower, always with an eye on the future of his beloved country, wrote: "No nation is drunken where wine is cheap and none sober where the dearness of wine substitutes ardent spirits as the common beverage."[13]

Not every writer, however, viewed wine as the fount of human well-being. Francois de Salignac de la Mothe Fenelon wrote at about the same time Dom Perignon was drinking stars: "Some of the most dreadful mischiefs that afflict mankind proceed from wine; it is the cause of disease, quarrels, sedition, idleness, aversion to labour, and every species of domestic disorder."[14]

William Jennings Bryan, secretary of state in Woodrow Wilson's cabinet, was another person who did not view wine as an essential component of the good life. On at least one occasion, he made his feelings quite clear. The conversation, unfortunately, has not been preserved, but it is known that he shocked the Washington diplomatic corps at a state dinner for the British ambassador at which he served grape juice instead of wine.[15] If the bishops of the Episcopal church had been present at the dinner, they would have sided with the British ambassador. In 1886 the church's House of Bishops resolved that the use of unfermented grape juice "as the lawful and the proper wine of the Holy Eucharist is unwarranted by the example of our Lord and an unauthorized departure from the custom of the Catholic Church."[16]

10. Ibid., 25.
11. Church, *American Guide,* 61.
12. Bespaloff, *Fireside Book,* 21.
13. Schoonmaker, *Encyclopedia of Wine,* 191.
14. John Bartlett, *Familiar Quotations* (Boston: Little, Brown, and Company, 1951), 1166.
15. Leon D. Adams, *The Wines of America,* 148.
16. Schoonmaker, *Encyclopedia of Wine,* 279.

Perhaps Shakespeare had the balanced view: "Good wine is a good familiar creature if it be well used." (*Othello,* act 2, scene 3)

Wine has been a favorite subject of poets from the ancient Greeks to modern times. The poem most often quoted in wine books is the one inspired by Nicholas Longworth's wine and written by Henry Wadsworth Longfellow. Longworth, great-grandfather of the Longworth who married Alice Roosevelt, was a successful vintner in Ohio early in the last century. After sampling his sparkling Catawba, Longfellow wrote:

> Very good in its way
> Is the Verzenay,
> Or the Sillery soft and creamy;
> But Catawba wine
> Has a taste more divine,
> More dulcet, delicious, and dreamy.[17]

The poetry may not be of prize-winning caliber, but it is doubtful that the wine was, either.

The most eloquent tribute to a wine may well be one that contains no spoken words. It has been traditional for French army units to salute when they pass the vineyard of the magnificent Clos de Vougeot.[18]

And finally, if you can't think what to say when a friend asks your opinion of a not-very-good wine, you might borrow comments occasionally heard at Wine Advisory Board tastings:

"It pours nicely."

"It stands well in the glass."

---

17. Adams, *Wines of America,* 94.
18. Lichine, *New Encyclopedia,* 523.

Pronunciation Guide

EVERY area of specialized interest has a jargon all its own. The language of wine is an international jargon. The name of a wine may have one pronunciation in one country and a different pronunciation, with perhaps different spelling, in another country. Wine encyclopedias often do not agree on pronunciations or spellings.

This is an informal, nonacademic guide. If you use these pronunciations you may not score an *A* in a language class, but wine shop clerks and sommeliers will understand you.

Ahr (*are*)
Alicante Bouschet (*ah-lee-*KAHN-*tay boo-shay*)
Aligote (*ah-lee-go-*TAY)
Aloxe-Corton (*ahl-ohss-*COR-*tawn*)
Anjou (*awn-zhoo*)
appellation controlee (*ah-pell-*AH-*see-ahn cahn-troll-*AY)
Asti Spumante (AHS-*tea spoo-*MAHN-*tay*)
auslese (*ous-lay-zuh*)
Aux Malconsorts (*oh mal-cahn-sor*)

Baco Noir (*bah-co nwar*)
Baden (*bahd'n*)
Barbaresco (*bar-bar-*ESS-*co*)
Barbera (*bar-*BEAR-*ah*)
Bardolino (*bar-do-*LEAN-*o*)
Barolo (*bar-oh-lo*)
Barsac (*bar-sack*)
Batard Montrachet (BAT-*tarr mon-rah-*SHAY)
Beaujolais (BO-*zho-lay*)
Beaune (*bone*)
Beau Site (*bo seat*)
beerenauslese (*bear-en-ous-lay-zuh*)
Bergstrasse (*bairg-strah-suh*)

Bernkastel (*behrn-kahss-tel*)

Beychevelle (*baysh-vel*)

Blanchots (*blahn-sho*)

Boal (*boo-al*)

Bordeaux (*bor*-DO)

Botrytis cinerea (*bo-try-tiss sin-air-eh-ah*)

Boucheres (*boo-shair*)

Bougros (*boo-gro*)

Bourgueil (*boor-goy*)

Brauneberg (*brown-uh-bairg*)

Brouilly (BREW-*ye*)

Cabernet (*cab-air-nay*)

Cabernet Franc (*cab-air-nay fran*)

Cabernet Sauvignon (*cab-air-nay so-ve-nyon*)

Cahors (*kah*-OR)

Canaiolo (*kah-na*-YO-*lo*)

Carignan (*car-ree*-NYAN)

carte de vin (*kart duh van*)

Chablis (*shahb-lee*)

chacun a son gout (*shakuh ah sawh goo*)

Chalonnais (*shah-lo-nay*)

Chambertin (SHAHM-*bair-tan*)

Champagne (*sham-pain*)

Chardonnay (SHAHR-*do-nay*)

Charmes (*shahrm*)

Chassagne (*shass*-AN-YA)

chateau (*shot*-OH)

Chateauneuf-du-Pape (*shot-to*-NUFF *dew* POP)

Chauche Gris (*show-shah gree*)

Chenas (*shay-nass*)

Chenin Blanc (*shay-nan blahn*)

Cheval Blanc (*shev-al blahn*)

Chevalier Montrachet (*shev*-AL-*yea mon-rah*-SHAY)

Chianti (*key*-AHN-*tee*)

Chinon (*shee-nawn*)

Chiroubles (*shee-roobl*)

Climens (*clee-mense*)

Clos de Vougeot (*clo duh* voo-*zho*)

Cockburn (*coh-burn*)

Colombard (*co-lahm-bar*)

Condrieu (CAHN-*dree-uh*)

Corton (*cor-tahn*)

Corton Charlemagne (*cor-tahn charl*-MAHN)

Cote de Brouilly (*coht duh brew-ye*)

Cote d'Or (*coht dor*)

Cotes-du-Rhone (*coht-dew-rohn*)

Cote Rotie (*coht ro-tee*)

Coutet (coo-*tay*)

cuvee (*coo-vay*)

denominazione di origine controllata (*de-no-me-nat-syo-ne de o-re-je-ne kon-troh-la-ta*)

denominazione di origine controllata e garantita (*de-no-me-nat-syo-ne de o-re-je-ne kon-troh-la-ta e gah-rahn-tee-ta*)

Dijon (*dee-zhon*)

Dubonnet (*doo-bahn-nay*)

Duriff (*doo-reef*)

Echezeaux (EH-*shay-zoh*)

edelzwicker (*eh-dell-zvick-er*)

eiswein (*ice-vine*)

Eltz (*eltz*)

Epernay (*a-pair-nay*)

Erbach (*air-bahk*)

escargot (*ess-kar-goh*)

Figeac (FEE-*jack*)

Filhot (FEE-*yo*)

fino (*fee-no*)

Fleurie (*flur-ree*)

Folle Blanche (*fahl blahnsh*)

Franken (*frank-n*)

Frascati (*frahs*-SCOT-*ee*)
frizzante (*free*-ZAHN-*tay*)

Gamay (*gah-may*)
Garganega (*gar*-GAHN-*eh-ga*)
Gattinara (*gah-tee*-NAH-*ra*)
Genevrieres (*zhan*-vree-air)
Gewurztraminer (*ge*-VERTZ-*tram-me-ner*)
Ghemme (GHEM-*may*)
Gironde (*zhe-rahnd*)
Graach (*grack*)
grand cru (*grahn kroo*)
Grands Echezeaux (*grahnz* EH-*shay-zo*)
Graves (*grahv*)
Grenache (*greh*-NAHSH)
Grenouilles (*greh*-NOO-*y*)
Grignolino (*green-yo*-LEAN-*no*)
Groslot (*gro-lo*)
Grillet (GREE-*yay*)

Hallgarten (HALL-*gar-ten*)
Hattenheim (HOT-*ten-hime*)
Haut-Brion (*oh*-BREE-*ahn*)
Hermitage (AIR-*me-tazh*)

Julienas (*zule*-YEA-*nahss*)
Jurancon (ZHOOR-*ahn-sahn*)

kabinett (*cab-ee*-NET)

Lafite-Rothschild (*la-feet-raht-sheel*)
Lambrusco (*lom*-BRUCE-*co*)
La Tache (*la tash*)
Latour (*la-toor*)
La Tour-Blanche (*la toor-blahnsh*)

Les Clos (*lay clo*)
Les Preuses (*lay prooz*)
Lessona (*less-*SOHN*-ah*)
Les Suchots (*lay soo-sho*)
Liebfraumilch (*leeb-frow-milsh*)
Lirac (LEE-*rack*)
Loire (*lwahr*)
Louis Beauchant (*loo-e bo-shan*)

Maconnais (MAC-*cahn-nay*)
Madiran (*mad-dee-rahn*)
maitre de chai (*metr duh shay*)
Malbec (*mal-beck*)
Margaux (*mar-go*)
Markobrunn (MAR-*ko*-BROON)
Marquis de Goulaine (*mar-kee duh goo-lane*)
Marsala (*mar-sah-la*)
Medoc (MAY-*dahk*)
Melon (*muh-lawn*)
Merlot (*mair-lo*)
Meursault (MERE-*so*)
mis en bouteilles au domaine (or) chateau (*me zan boo-tee-ya o doe-men* (or) *shot-*OH)
Mittlerhein (*mit-tel-rine*)
Montrachet (*mahn-rah-*SHAY)
Morgon (MOR-*gahn*)
Mosel (*moz'l*)
Mosel-Saar-Ruwer (*moz'l-sahr-roo-ver*)
Moselle (*mo-*ZELL)
Moulin-a-vent (MOO-*lahn-ah-*VAHN)
Moulis (*moo-lee*)
Mouton-Rothschild (MOO-*tahn-raht-sheel*)
Muller-Thurgau (MOOL-*ar* TOOR-*gow*)
Muscadelle (MUHS-*cah*-DEL)
Muscadet (*muhs-cah-day*)
Muscat (*mus-kat*)
Musigny (MOOS-*een-ye*)

Nahe (*nah*)
Nebbiolo (*neb-be-*o*-lo*)
negociant (*ne-gos-yan*)
Nouveau Beaujolais (*noo-vo* BO-*zho-lay*)
Nuits-St.-Georges (*nwee-san-zhorzh*)

oloroso (*o-lo-*RO-*so*)
Orvieto (*or-vee-*AY-*to*)

Palatinate (*pal-*LAT-*teen-ate*)
pates (*pa-tay*)
Pauillac (*pah-yack*)
Pedro Ximenez (PAY-*dro hee-*MAY-*nays*)
Perrieres (*per-ree-*AIR)
petillant (*pay-tee-yahn*)
Petite Sirah (*puh-tee see-rah*)
Petrus (*pay-trooss*)
Piesporter (*pees-port-air*)
Pineau de la-Loire (*pee-no duh la-lwahr*)
Pinot Blanc (PEE-*no blahn*)
Pinot Meunier (*pee-no-muhn-yea*)
Pinot Noir (PEE-*no nwahr*)
Pomerol (*pahm-may-rahl*)
Pommard (PO-*mar*)
Pouilly-Fuisse (POO-*ye* FWEE-*say*)
Pouilly-Fume (POO-*ye* FEW-*may*)
pourriture noble (POO-*ree-tew'r* NO-*b'l*)
premier grand cru (*preem-yea grahn krew*)
primitivo (*pree-muh-*TEE-*vo*)
Puligny (POO-*lean-ye*)

qualitatswein (*quahl-ah-tahts-vine*)
qualitatswein mit pradikat (*qual-ah-tahts-vine mit prah-dee-cot*)

Rauenthal (ROU-*en-tahl*)

Reinhartshausen (RINE-*harts*-HOW-*zen*)

retsina (*ret-see-nah*)

Rheingau (RINE-*gow*)

Rheinhessen (*rine-hess-en*)

Rheinpfalz (RINE-*pfahlts*)

Richebourg (REESH-*boorg*)

Riesling (REECE-*ling*)

Rieussec (REE-*oo-sec*)

Rioja (*ree-o-ha*)

de Rochefort (*duh* ROSH-*for*)

Romanee-Conti (RO-*mah*-NAY-CAHN-*tee*)

Romanee-St.-Vivant (RO-*mah*-NAY- *san-vee*-VAHN)

rosé (*ro*-ZAY)

Ruwer (*roo-ver*)

Saar (*sahr*)

St. Amour (*sant ah-moor*)

St. Emilion (sant *a*-MEE-*lee-ahn*)

Saint-Estephe (*sant-ee*-STEFF)

Saint-Julien (*san*-ZHOE-*lee-an*)

Sancerre (*sahn-sair*)

San Gioveto (*san jo*-VAY-*to*)

Saone (*sone*)

Sauternes (*saw-tairn*)

Sauvignon (SO-*veen-yawn*)

schloss (*shlahss*)

Semillon (SAY-*me-yahn*)

Sercial (SAIR-*see-al*)

Soave (SWA-*vay*)

solera (*so*-LAIR-*ah*)

sommelier (*so-mel-yay*)

spatlese (SHPATE-*lay-zuh*)

spritzig (SHPRIT-*sikh*)

spumante (*spoo*-MAHN-*tay*)

Sylvaner (*sil*-VAHN-*ner*)

Syrah (*see-rah*)

tafelwein (*tah-fel-vine*)

Tavel (*tah*-VEL)

Touraine (*tou*-RAIN)

Trebbiano (*treb-bee-*AH-*no*)

Trier (TREE-*er*)

trockenbeerenauslese (TRAHK-*ken-bear-en-ous-lay-zuh*)

Urzig (*oort-sig*)

Valmur (*val-moor*)

Valpolicella (*vahl-po-lee-*CHEL-*la*)

Valtellina (*vahl-tel-*LEEN-*na*)

Vaudesir (VO-*day-zeer*)

Verdicchio (*vair-*DEE-*kee-o*)

Vieux Chateau Certan (*vee-*YUH *shot-*OH SAIR-*tahn*)

vins delimites de qualite superieure (*van day-*LEE-*me-tay duh* CAHL-*lee-tay soo-*PAY-*ree-*AIR)

viognier (*vee-*ON-*yay*)

Vollrads (*fahl-rahdz*)

Vosne-Romanee (*vone-*RO-*may-nay*)

Vouvray (*voo-vray*)

Wehlen (VAY-*len*)

Wurttemberg (VERT-*ahm-bairg*)

d'Yquem (*dee-kem*)

Zell (*tsell*)

Zeltingen (*tsel-ting-en*)

zwicker (ZVICK-*er*)

I N D E X

The page numbers of principal references are shown in *italic* type

1 0 6

Jug wines, 5, *72–76*
Julienas, 29
Fr. Juniper Serra, 31
Jurancon, 85

Kabinett, 62–63
Keenan Winery, 23
Kenwood Vineyards, 37
Koblenz, 24
Kool-Aid, 88–89
Kosher wines, 48
Kressmann, Edouard, xi

Labels, 50–67
  French, 55–61
  German, 61–64
  Italian, 64–67
  United States, 50–55
Ladoucette Pouilly-Fume, 41
Lambrusco, 5, *30,* 47, 66, 89
Lancers, 45
La Romanee, 18
La Tache, 18
Leroy Vineyards, 19
Les Clos, 21
Les Preuses, 21
Lessona, 32
Les Suchots, 18
Lichine, Alex, xi, 9, 52
Liebfraumilch, 62
Light wines, 75–76
Lirac, 61
Livermore Valley Vineyards, 31, 35
Loire Valley, 17, 37, 39, 41, 56, *60–61*
Lombardy, 32
Longfellow, Henry Wadsworth, 93
Long vineyards, 23
Longworth, Nicholas, 93
Los Angeles, 31
Los Hermanos Vineyards, 76
Louis Beauchant, 39
Louis Martini Winery, 28, 40, 74, 86–87

Macon, 22
Maconnais, 58
Macconnais Blanc, 21
Madeira, 71
Madiran, 85–86
Malbec, 30
Malinara, 66
Malmsey, 71, 91

Manzanilla, 69
Margaux, 58. *See also* Chateau Margaux
Markobrunn, 24
Marquis de Goulaine, 39
Marsala, 64, *71*
Mateus, 45
Mayacamus Vineyards, 17
Medoc district, 16, 56–58
Melon, 39, 61
Mendocino County, 23
Merlot, 17, 58
Meursault Vineyards, 21–22, 40
Mexico, 31
Mission, 31
Missouri Riesling, 26
Mittelrhein, 62
Moet et Chandon, 60
Monterey County, 23, 37
Monterey Vineyards, 41–42, 44, 74
Montevina Vineyards, 36, 42, 53
Montrachet Vineyards, 21–23, 40, 59
Morgon, 29
Moselle, 23–25, 62
Mosel-Saar-Ruwer, 62
Mother Vineyard Scuppernong, 49
Moulin-a-Vent, 29
Moulis, 58
Mountain Red, 54
Mount Veeder Winery, 18, 23, 36, 37
Mouton-Rothchild Vineyards, 17
Muller-Thurgau, *39,* 51, 62
Mumm, 60
Muscadelle, 26, 43
Muscadet, *39,* 60–61
Muscadine, 49
Muscat, 26, *39–40,* 66
Muscat Amabile, 40
Muscat Canelli, 39
Muscat de Frontignan, 31
Muscat of Alexandria, 40
Musigny, 18, 21
Must, 9, 12–13, 25

Nahe, 62
Napa Valley, 23, 28
Napa Gamay, 28
Nebbiolo, 31–32
Negrara, 66
New Mexico, 45
New York, 21, 23, 26, 46, 48, 54
New Zealand, 45
Niagra, 49

About the Authors

BOTH authors are native Iowans. Both have traveled widely in the wine regions of the world. Both are members of the Iowa Wine Advisory Board.

KENNETH MACDONALD is a journalist. He was editor of the *Des Moines Register and Tribune* for more than twenty years and publisher of those newspapers for ten. Although he doesn't claim credit for it, the newspapers during his tenure were awarded more Pulitzer prizes than any other newspaper except the *New York Times.* He was president of the American Society of Newspaper Editors and first vice-president of The Associated Press. With his wife, Helen, he has traveled for the Des Moines newspapers in Europe, Asia, and the Americas. He has been an amateur student of wine for twenty-five years.

TOM THROCKMORTON is a surgeon. Trained at the Mayo Clinic, he is Associate Clinical Professor of Surgery at the University of Iowa and coordinator of the surgical residency training program at the Iowa Methodist Medical Center in Des Moines. He bought his first full case of wine thirty years ago and has been learning about wine ever since. He and his wife, Jean, have repeatedly traveled the wine roads of France and California, and he is well known to many of the vintners of those areas. He is one of three Iowa members of the *Confrerie des Chevaliers du Tastevin, Clos Vougeot Chapitre,* and one of two Iowa members of the *Commanderie de Bordeaux.* His interests are broad. In addition to membership in national surgical societies, he is past president of the American Daffodil Society and a winner of the Peter Barr Cup of the Royal Horticultural Society of England.

Drink Thy Wine With a Merry Heart makes a
great gift for friends, relatives and business/professional associates.
To order additional copies of this comprehensive guide to the basics
of buying, serving, and enjoying wine, check with your local
bookstore or use the handy order form below.

ORDER FORM

Please send me _____copies of DRINK THY WINE WITH A
MERRY HEART, #0476-0, at $7.50 per copy postpaid.

Ordering Information:
_____Payment enclosed.

     $_____TOTAL AMOUNT ENCLOSED.

_____Credit card payment.

     _____VISA®   _____MasterCard™

_____   _____

Card number   Expiration date

_____Send information on other books of general interest from ISU
     Press

Name_____

Address_____

City/State/Zip _____

Telephone__(_____)_____

              Send to: **Iowa State University Press**
                      Marketing Department
                      2121 South State Avenue
                      Ames, Iowa 50010